BUST! OR? TRUST

A Kids' Mystery Book

By **Small Wardour**
Illustrated by **Sam Peet**

words&pictures

To all our Chief Detectives, we make a great team! – S.W.

For Sigrid – S.P.

First published in 2025 by words & pictures,
an imprint of The Quarto Group.
1 Triptych Place, London,
SE1 9SH, United Kingdom
T (0)20 7700 6700 F (0)20 7700 8066
www.quarto.com

EEA Representation, WTS Tax d.o.o., Žanova ulica 3, 4000 Kranj, Slovenia

Editor: Alice Hobbs
Senior Commissioning Editor: Catharine Robertson
Designer: Victoria Vassiades
Senior Designer: Sarah Chapman-Suire
Creative Director: Malena Stojić
Associate Publisher: Holly Willsher
Production Manager: Nikki Ingram

A catalogue record for this book is available from the British Library.

ISBN: 978-1-83600-171-3

9 8 7 6 5 4 3 2 1

Manufactured in Malaysia PC062025

MIX
Paper | Supporting responsible forestry
FSC® C007207

Bust or Trust is created by Small Wardour, children's audio experts and producers of award-winning podcasts such as *Super Great Kids' Stories*, *My First Podcast*, *Bullfrogs & Lizards*, and *Bust or Trust* – a fun kids' mystery show full of jokes, quirky facts and critical thinking, hosted by buster Athena Kugblenu and truster Tiernan Douieb.

The *Bust or Trust* book wouldn't have been possible without the dedication and creativity of Bust or Trust HQ: **Carla Herbertson**, **David Smith**, **Athena Kugblenu**, **Tiernan Douieb**, **Rachel Matthews**, **Lucy Wroe** and **Tom Berry**. Special thanks to **Shannon Cullen** and the **words & pictures** team as well as **Danni Haughan**, **Sara Azmy** and **The Philosophy Foundation**.

Be sure to catch *Bust or Trust* and all Small Wardour podcasts on your favourite podcast platform!

BUST! OR? TRUST

A Kids' Mystery Book

By **Small Wardour**

Illustrated by
Sam Peet

words&pictures

CONTENTS

THE LEGEND OF KING ARTHUR

THE CURSED TOMBS OF EGYPT

BIGFOOT

THE CURIOUS CASE OF AMELIA EARHART

OKIKU THE HAUNTED DOLL

THE LOST CITY OF ATLANTIS

RASPUTIN'S MYSTICAL POWERS

THE CRYSTAL SKULLS

THE LOCH NESS MONSTER

THE DEMON DANCING PLAGUE OF EUROPE

Look up tricky words in the dictionary at the back of the book.

CALLING ALL CHIEF DETECTIVES!

Are you ready to unravel the world's greatest mysteries? Pick up your magnifying glass and put on your detective caps, because you're about to enter the wacky, case-cracking world of Bust or Trust!

The Legend of King Arthur

Bigfoot

The Cursed Tombs of Egypt

The Curious Case of Amelia Earhart

Following on from the award-winning *Bust or Trust* podcast, we're proud to get you involved in more mystery magic. In this book, you will find 10 bizarre, unusual cases from all over the world. These baffling puzzles have left historians and scientists scratching their heads for years . . . which is where *you* come in!

From Bigfoot to the Lost City of Atlantis, you'll be exploring legendary people, strange events, mythical creatures, magical places and otherworldly tales. We'll give you the case, and you – our Chief Detective – will decide whether to **BUST** or **Trust** it!

Okiku the Haunted Doll

Rasputin's Mystical Powers

The Loch Ness Monster

The Lost City of Atlantis

The Crystal Skulls

The Demon Dancing Plague of Europe

Meet Buster & Truster!

But don't worry, you won't be investigating alone! Detective Deputies Buster and Truster will be helping you along the way. Together, they will take you step-by-step through the details of each case and show you all the *evidence* you need to crack it! Be careful though, as Buster and Truster will also be trying to get you to believe *their* side of the story.

Evidence is information that gives you a reason to believe something is true.

INTRODUCING BUSTER BRAINS!

Why hello there, Chief Detective! My name is **BUSTER** and I'll be one of your Detective Deputies on this Bust or Trust journey. After you've seen all the evidence, I will present you with some myth-busting arguments to prove to you why every case is most definitely a *Bust* instead of a Trust!

Unlike Truster, I like to bust the myths with cold, hard evidence and scientific explanations. While I'm a fan of all weird and wonderful stories, that's what I believe these cases are – just really cool *stories*!

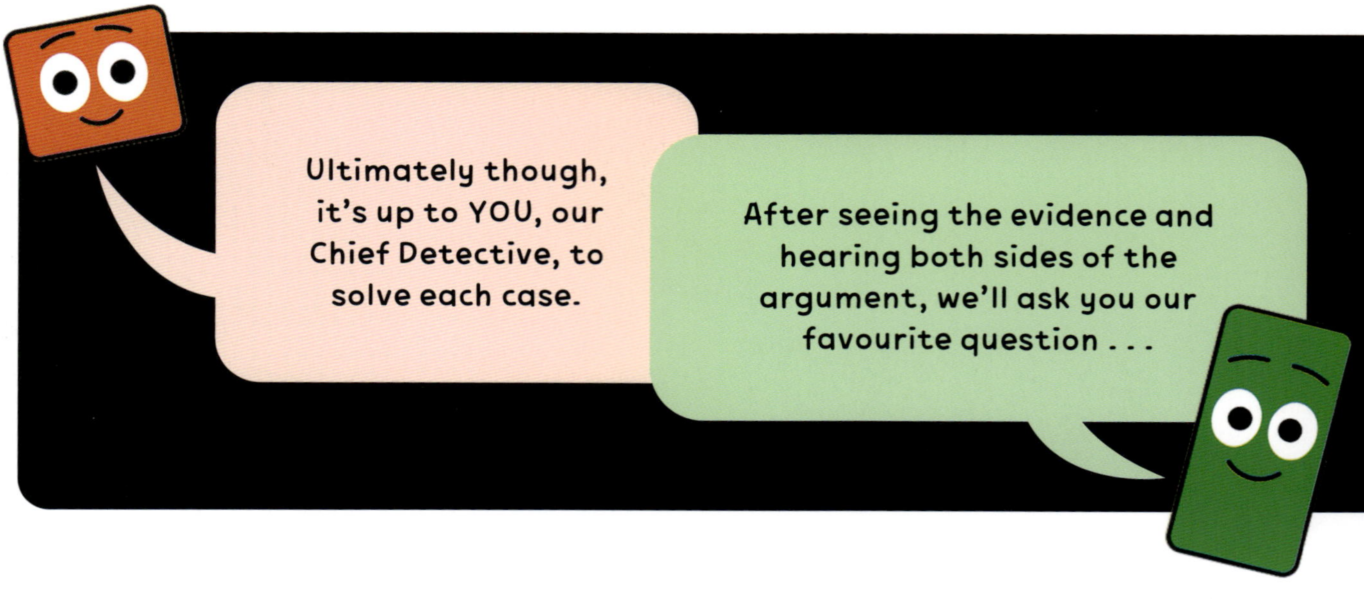

Ultimately though, it's up to YOU, our Chief Detective, to solve each case.
After seeing the evidence and hearing both sides of the argument, we'll ask you our favourite question . . .

INTRODUCING TRUSTER TRUTH!

Okay, okay! But not everyone thinks the same way, and Buster isn't your only Detective Deputy! Hi there, Chief Detective, I'm **TRUSTER**, and I will be giving you my side of the argument on each case. From the weird to the wonderful, the truth is out there!

Remember, just because something *sounds* strange, it doesn't mean it can't be true. Even Buster has to admit, there are thousands of things in the universe we don't yet know or understand! Like, are aliens out there? Is time travel possible? And if dragons NEVER existed, then why do so many countries have stories about them? Hmmmm . . .

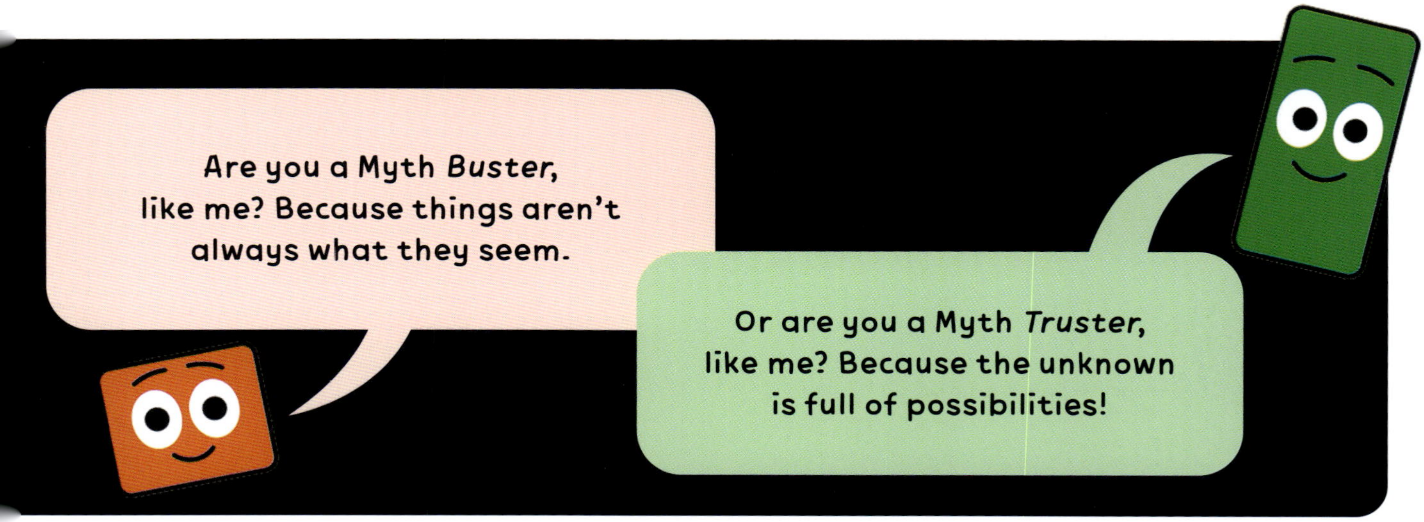

Are you a Myth *Buster*, like me? Because things aren't always what they seem.
Or are you a Myth *Truster*, like me? Because the unknown is full of possibilities!

HOW TO THINK LIKE A CHIEF DETECTIVE

As you investigate the cases in this book, you'll uncover fun facts, discover new words and read silly stories! You'll also be introduced to some important detective skills. Armed with these, there is no mystery too big or too strange for you to solve!

At the end of every mystery, we're going to show you how to think like a Chief Detective! Don't worry – it's not that scary. It just means we're going to help you Bust or Trust the case through fun activities and thinking games! For each mystery, you'll use a particular detective skill (see box opposite) to help you crack the case.

This is because we want to help YOU analyse the evidence and seek different points of view. This is called *critical thinking*. By giving you the detective skills, you can then make your own decision about what you believe – you're the Chief Detective here, after all!

Critical thinking is the act of questioning our own opinions and using reason to solve problems.

DETECTIVE SKILLS

In this book, you'll use five detective skills:

1. **Weighing the Evidence:** This skill will help you decide which evidence to believe.

2. **Thinking in Grey:** This skill is all about asking, 'Is the answer always one thing or another, or is it sometimes somewhere in between?'

3. **Doing Independent Research:** Use this skill to find good, reliable information by yourself.

4. **Evaluating Testimony:** This skill is all about evaluating, or judging, the things that people say.

5. **Checking for Personal Bias:** Use this skill to separate feelings from facts!

Are you ready,
Chief Detective?
Let's **BUST** or **TRUST**!

The Detective Dictionary

Every case takes us to mysterious new places and introduces us to interesting detective words. But don't worry, we'll explain everything along the way. Whenever there's an important word, there will be a little circle explaining exactly what that word means. AND if you ever get stuck, there's a handy Detective Dictionary at the back of the book to help you out!

How This Book Works

So before we start, let's just recap how this book works. For each case . . .

✦ First, the mystery is introduced, with a handy detective timeline of key events.

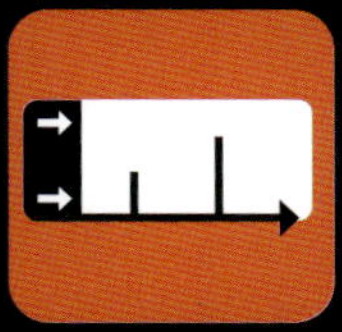

✦ Next, you're shown three pieces of important evidence. These could be old photos, eyewitness accounts or the results of scientific tests.

✦ Buster and Truster each present arguments for their side of the case.

✦ You learn a detective skill.

✦ Finally, YOU solve the case!

THE LEGEND OF KING ARTHUR

Our very first case is world famous and historical! It's about the knight, warrior and famous ruler of Britain, King Arthur Pendragon of Camelot. Or rather, the *alleged* ruler of Britain. That's right, we're investigating whether King Arthur was a real historical figure, or just a story.

King Arthur was a legendary figure who supposedly ruled Britain in the late 5th to early 6th centuries, after the Romans left. Back then, Britain was quite different to today. It was ruled by various Celtic tribes, who were known together as the Britons. King Arthur was said to have united these tribes under one ruler, and helped them to fight off invasions from the Saxons of Northern Germany.

→ TIMELINE →

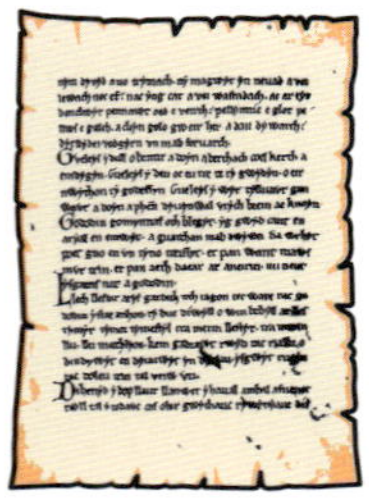

7th–11th centuries

Arthur is mentioned in the Welsh poem *Y Gododdin*.

828

King Arthur crops up again in *History of the Britons*.

1135

Geoffrey of Monmouth writes about Arthur in *The History of the Kings of Britain*.

Swords and Sorcery

Most people know King Arthur from the famous stories that have been told about him in books, films, TV shows and plays, all across the world. In one tale, the young Arthur pulls a magical sword from a stone. The sword, named Excalibur, could only be removed by the rightful king . . . or so the legend goes.

Other famous stories introduce us to King Arthur's castle of Camelot, his wife, Guinevere, his sorceress sister, Morgan Le Fay, and the good wizard Merlin. Legend says that Arthur held meetings with his knights around a huge circular table known as the Round Table. In some stories, 12 knights sat around it, while in other stories it seated 150 – that's one big table!

Man or Myth?

This is part of the problem with the legends about King Arthur. Often the details of the stories aren't quite the same, which makes it very hard to prove if Arthur was a real person or not. And with ancient stories, so much gets lost over the years that it's hard to check what's true and what's not. Like, for instance, who made Excalibur? Where was Camelot? And, most importantly, what happened to that enormous round table?

Now it's up to you, Chief Detective, to decide whether King Arthur was a real king or more of a medieval myth?

Arthur and Guinevere's tomb is reportedly discovered.

1191

A scholar describes visiting Arthur's tomb.

1530s

An archaeological dig in Cornwall uncovers a stone with the word 'Artognue' carved into it.

1998

Turn the page to keep reading and find out about these events, and more!

THE EVIDENCE

Okay, Chief Detective, let's put on our detective hats and find out whether King Arthur was a man . . . or a myth!

FIRST PIECE OF EVIDENCE:

The History of the Kings of Britain, 1135

There are quite a few old books that mention King Arthur, and one of the oldest and most famous is *The History of the Kings of Britain*, which was written around 1135 by Geoffrey of Monmouth, a Welsh monk. His account of King Arthur includes many of the parts of the story we know today, such as Camelot and the infamous sword Excalibur.

A lot of Geoffrey's book is quite fantastical, which means it contains things that aren't real, like magic and dragons – and there's no proof that they existed in 5th- or 6th-century Britain!

HOWEVER, Geoffrey translated his book from another ancient book into Latin, so there's always the chance that he got a few bits wrong along the way.

SECOND PIECE OF EVIDENCE:

Archaeological digs at Tintagel, Cornwall, 1930 & 1998

Geoffrey of Monmouth's book mentions Tintagel in Cornwall as the place where Arthur was born. And get this – a big archaeological dig in 1930 revealed that there *was* a large settlement there in the 5th to 7th centuries, which is around the time Arthur was meant to have been alive!

Then, in 1998, archaeologists discovered a large stone slab in Tintagel with the mysterious word 'Artognue' carved on it. We don't know for certain what that word means, but some people have argued it's an old way of saying 'Arthur' and the stone was there to show people they were in the king's realm.

THIRD PIECE OF EVIDENCE:

Reported discovery of Arthur and Guinevere's skeletons, 1191

Even if we aren't sure where King Arthur was born, we might know where he was buried!

Guinevere was Arthur's queen and true love, and it seems the two were buried together – how romantic! In 1191, priest and historian Gerald of Wales wrote in a book that the couple's bodies had been discovered by monks in the famous Glastonbury Abbey. He even described visiting the tomb himself, so we have an *eyewitness* account!

> *. . . buried deep in the earth in a hollow oak and deposited becomingly in a marble tomb. Here too a leaden cross, placed under a stone, which I have seen, for I have touched these letters carved there, contained: 'Here lies buried the glorious king Arthur and Guinevere his second wife in the Isle of Avalon.'*

Hundreds of years later, in the 1530s, a scholar called John Leland also visited the tomb. He described it as being made of black marble, with a crucifix. HOWEVER, the skeletons mysteriously disappeared in 1539. And today no trace of the tomb remains . . .

An *eyewitness* is a person who has seen something happen and can tell others about it.

THE MYTH BUSTER ARGUMENT

Okay, Chief Detective! Let's take a look at the evidence and see if you're a Myth Buster like me.

BUST ARGUMENT ONE:

Fact or fiction?

Geoffrey of Monmouth's book *The History of the Kings of Britain* contains one of the oldest and most well-known tales of King Arthur, but the fact is he wrote his history hundreds of years after Arthur even existed. It's almost a story of a story of a story!

While it was considered historically accurate back in the 16th century, since then it has been studied by lots of very smart people and is now largely considered to be historically unreliable.

Geoffrey never even said *himself* whether he believed the legend of King Arthur. Scholars now believe that he cobbled together lots of details from different historic British figures to make up one amazing Celtic superhero. It's very possible that Geoffrey of Monmouth was just a brilliant storyteller!

BUST ARGUMENT TWO:

Stone-cold evidence

It's true that archaeologists discovered a town in Tintagel that existed at the same time as King Arthur. And it's also true that there was a stone slab found there with the word 'Artognue' carved into it. However, not everyone believes that Artognue means 'Arthur'. Celtic expert John Koch thinks the word actually means 'bear-knowledge'. So, nothing to do with Arthur at all!

So, despite the existence of the settlement and the stone, there's no actual proof that King Arthur ever lived there.

BUST ARGUMENT THREE:

Now you see it . . . now you don't!

Remember those remains of Arthur and Guinevere that were supposedly found in a tomb in Glastonbury Abbey? Well, many historians think this was a *fraud* carried out by the monks of Glastonbury Abbey. In 1184, just before the visit by Gerald of Wales, there had been a fire at the abbey. What better way to raise money for repairs than a tourist attraction of a king's bones? The timing is very suspicious!

And let's not forget that NO fragments of the tomb or the bones are known to survive. So, it's hard to prove that they ever existed at all.

Fraud means tricking someone, usually to make money.

THE MYTH TRUSTER ARGUMENT

Okay, Buster, you've made some great ARTHURments. But there's always more to consider!

TRUST ARGUMENT ONE:

Tale as old as time

Geoffrey of Monmouth's book from around 1135 is one of the oldest and most well-known histories of King Arthur, but it's not the only one! King Arthur also appears in an earlier book from 828 called *History of the Britons*, where he is described as a military leader fighting against Saxon invaders in the 5th to 6th centuries. He also pops up in the *Annals of Wales*, a collection of complicated Latin records believed to have been created in the 10th century.

Possibly the earliest ever mention of Arthur by name occurs in the Welsh poem *Y Gododdin*, which is believed to have been written between the 7th and 11th centuries. Now that's old! Arthur appears only very briefly though . . .

Logic tells us that anyone mentioned so many times through history must have existed in *some* way, doesn't it?

TRUST ARGUMENT TWO:

Here, there and everywhere

Tintagel and Glastonbury Abbey aren't the only real-life places that have been linked to Arthur. There's another place with a strong connection to him: Wales.

Geoffrey of Monmouth and another medieval writer called Chrétien de Troyes *both* placed Camelot, Arthur's chief court and castle, in Caerleon, South Wales.

Now, this is interesting because Arthur has other connections with Wales. Remember the Welsh poem, *Y Gododdin*? Plus, the legend of Arthur also appears in *The Mabinogion*, a collection of Welsh stories that are believed to have been passed down by word of mouth through the ages. With ALL of these Welsh links, don't you think it seems likely that Camelot was indeed in Caerleon and that a real-life King Arthur once lived there?

TRUST ARGUMENT THREE:

Round and round the table!

From books such as T. H. White's *Sword in the Stone*, to TV shows and films, King Arthur has had a big influence on British culture. And there are places named after him all over Britain, from Arthur's Stone (a massive burial chamber in Herefordshire) to King Arthur's Round Table (a huge earthwork in Cumbria that is thought to have got its name in the 17th century).

It would be strange for someone who never existed to have had such a big impact, surely?

So now we're handing it over to you, Chief Detective, to decide if the legend of King Arthur is foolproof fact or fantastical fiction!

What do YOU think? Are you a King Arthur Myth Buster?
Or a King Arthur Myth Truster?

WHAT DO YOU THINK?

Right, Chief Detective, now you've heard all the evidence, let's put a new detective skill to the test. For this mystery, let's explore how to WEIGH THE EVIDENCE!

CRACKING THE CASE

First, read the Detective Skill box on the right. Then ask yourself, is there a lot of evidence that he was a real-life person, or not so much? And do you think the evidence is of good quality, or not? Start by making a list of all the evidence, then for each piece of evidence, decide how reliable YOU think it is. How much strong, good-quality evidence is there that King Arthur existed?

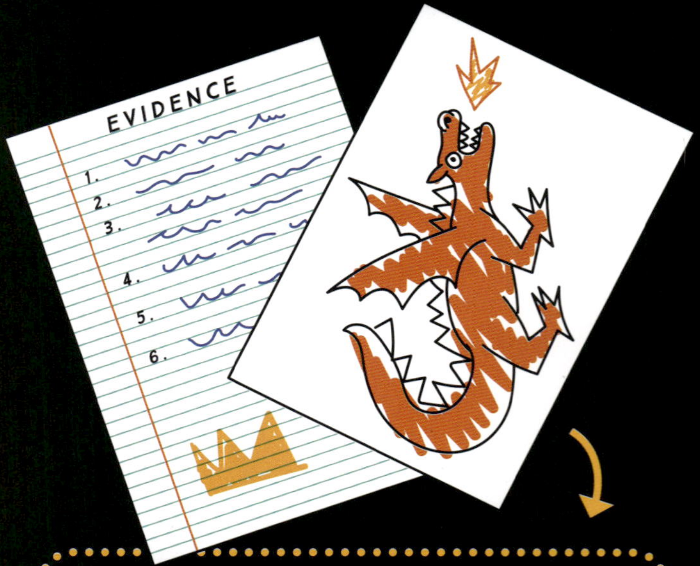

Then decide, are you a King Arthur **BUSTER** or a King Arthur **TRUSTER**?

DETECTIVE SKILL

Weigh the Evidence

To solve a mystery, we first need to look at the evidence. BUT beware, not all evidence is created equal! There are two key things to look out for:

1. **Quantity of Evidence:** This means how MUCH evidence we have. Imagine each piece of evidence is a block. One block isn't enough to build a tower – you need lots of blocks!

2. **Quality of Evidence:** This is how reliable the evidence is. For example, if you found King Arthur's skeleton, that would be pretty strong evidence that he existed. But if you hear a rumour that a friend of a friend claims to have seen King Arthur's skeleton, then that evidence isn't as strong.

Both the quantity *and* quality of evidence can help us figure out if we should believe in something.

In the castle of Camelot, King Arthur is preparing a surprise for his knights . . .

KNIGHTS OF CAMELOT! I WELCOME YOU TO MY CASTLE WHERE WE MEET AND SIT AS EQUALS. I BRING YOU . . . THE TRIANGULAR TABLE!
DO I HAVE TO SIT HERE? THE POINTY BIT IS DIGGING INTO ME.
THIS TABLE DOESN'T WORK DOES IT?
NO.

One week later . . .

One week later . . .

I BRING YOU, AND THIS HAD BETTER BE THE LAST TIME, THE ROUND TABLE!
OH, THIS IS GOOD. NO SHARP EDGES AND WE CAN ALL SEE EACH OTHER!

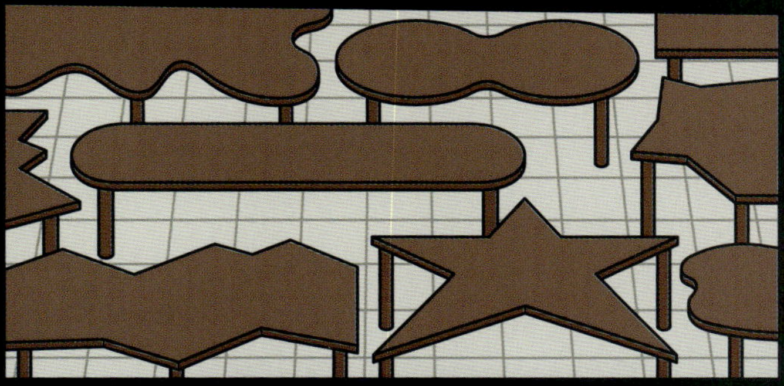

And that is the story of how the Round Table came to be. And how Arthur found himself with a chamber dedicated to strangely shaped tables . . .

BIGFOOT

Our second case is the legend of BIGFOOT! In case you haven't heard, Bigfoot – or Sasquatch as it is also known – is an infamous, huge ape-like creature that is said to stalk the wilderness of the USA . . .

The USA is a large country with a large population – 340 million people call it home. However, there are still some pretty big areas that don't have many people living in them, including vast forests and tall mountains. Perfect places for Bigfoot to hide!

People who claim to have spotted Bigfoot describe it as a creature that walks upright like a person, but is much, much bigger than any human you've ever known. It's reckoned to be 2–2.5 metres tall – that's like a grown-up carrying a toddler on their shoulders and the toddler wearing a really big hat!

TIMELINE

Five men claim they are attacked by huge, hairy 'mountain devils'.

1924

A newspaper reports on the discovery of giant 'Bigfoot' footprints.

1958

A tall, ape-like creature is captured on film.

1967

Hairy & Scary

Native American people have long told legends about strange, tall creatures and wild, hairy people lurking in the North American woods. The name 'Sasquatch' is actually believed to come from the Native American Salish word *sasq'ets* (pronounced sas-kets), which means 'wild man' or 'hairy man'.

What is interesting, though, is that it wasn't until 1958 that the name Bigfoot became popular. That year, an article in the *Humboldt Times* newspaper reported on some giant footprints found in Northern California. According to the story, locals who worked in the woods spotted the massive prints and called the creature that made them 'Bigfoot'. Since then, the name has stuck, and Bigfoot is now an American legend.

The Search for Bigfoot

Lots of people claim to have seen Bigfoot, and there have been countless newspaper reports and many, many TV shows dedicated to finding Bigfoot and catching it on camera. A large number of people have made it their life's mission to find definitive proof that Bigfoot exists.

And now it's up to you, our Chief Detective, to look through the evidence and analyse what you read. Only then will you be able to draw your final conclusions and find out whether you're a Myth Buster or a Myth Truster!

Researchers find a Bigfoot-shaped imprint in the mud.

2000

'Bigfoot' hair samples are tested.

2014

A couple spot a mysterious, ape-like creature from a train.

2023

Turn the page to keep reading and find out about these events, and more!

THE EVIDENCE

Okay, Chief Detective, let's investigate! We're going to show you three pieces of evidence and then you decide whether to Bust or Trust them. Read carefully and don't be afraid to change your mind. Are you ready? Let's go!

FIRST PIECE OF EVIDENCE:

Report from *The Oregonian*, a local Oregon newspaper, 1924

December 1924

The Oregonian

Fight with Big Apes Reported by Miners

Marlon Smith and his friends encountered the fabled mountain devils or mountain gorillas of Mount St. Helens this week, shooting one of them and being attacked throughout the night by rock bombardments of the beasts. The men . . . declared that they saw four of the huge animals, which were about 8 feet [2.5 metres] tall and walked upright.

This sounds like pretty definitive evidence, right? There are five named witnesses who all agree they saw what they thought was a mountain gorilla. And what's really interesting is that local Cowlitz Native Americans told the reporters that their elders had spoken of 'peculiar creatures' that sounded very similar to the 'mountain gorillas' that the witnesses spoke about! HOWEVER, no evidence for their story was ever found. The men said they shot and killed one of the creatures but local rangers could not find a body.

SECOND PIECE OF EVIDENCE:

Video recording, 1967

In 1967, two men, Roger Patterson and Bob Gimlin, were riding alongside Bluff Creek in Northern California when they saw a tall, hairy, ape-like creature standing on the far bank. Patterson had a camera on him, so he jumped off his horse to film it.

In the footage, you can clearly see what looks like a big gorilla person casually walking away towards the trees. The whole video lasts only one minute, before Bigfoot disappears into the woods. The men tried to track it, but lost the trail.

To many people, live footage of Bigfoot would be seen as convincing evidence! But not to a zoologist called Bernard Heuvelmans. He reckoned the creature must be someone in a suit because its fur was too neat and its movements were far too calm, especially considering it was being chased by two men on horses.

THIRD PIECE OF EVIDENCE:

Cast of Bigfoot, 2000

Chief Detective, we have – and this is so exciting – a cast of a Bigfoot! Or at least, a cast made of what is *supposedly* a Bigfoot. In 2000, researchers on a Bigfoot Field Researchers Organization (BFRO) expedition near Mount Adams, in Washington state, USA, were filming for a TV series called *Animal X*, when they discovered an imprint in the mud of what looked like a very large human lying on its side. So, they decided to make a plaster cast (a copy made in plaster) of it.

Several scientists who've studied the cast say the imprint was very likely made by an elk, a deer-like animal that is very common in forests in North America. But there are also several other scientists who are convinced it was made by Bigfoot. However, there was no other evidence at the scene – no hair, claw marks or even poo!

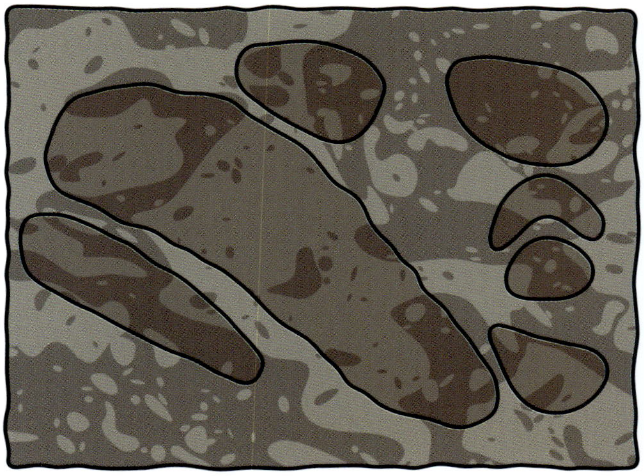

THE MYTH BUSTER ARGUMENT

Okay, Chief Detective! Let's take a look at the evidence and see if you're a Bigfoot Myth Buster like me!

BUST ARGUMENT ONE:

Eye spy!

Usually lots of eyewitnesses make a story more likely to be true. Still, it's difficult to decide how reliable these eyewitnesses are. People have made up *hoaxes* about all sorts of things, and for all sorts of reasons – money, attention, fame and sometimes just for fun! It's also been proven that even when someone thinks that they're telling the truth, often it's just their memory playing tricks on them. In other words, just because someone genuinely *thinks* they saw Bigfoot, it doesn't mean they actually did!

BUST ARGUMENT TWO:

Bigfoot bias!

It's worth considering that some of the people who discovered the evidence we've shown you are a little . . . *biased*. In other words, they were always going to be a Myth Truster! Think about it. The muddy imprint of Bigfoot was found by Bigfoot researchers for their TV series. Hmmm . . . seems a little suspicious that they *wanted* to find proof that Bigfoot exists – and then suddenly they did!

Bias is when what we *want* to believe has an influence on what we *do* believe.

A *hoax* is when someone is tricked into believing something to be true.

BUST ARGUMENT THREE:

It's all allegedly!

The word *allegedly* means that something hasn't been proven. No one has been able to prove that Bigfoot exists. Many experts who've examined the film footage from 1967 and the Bigfoot cast from 2000 have claimed it's all a hoax. In fact, most scientists who've looked at the evidence argue that there isn't enough proof that Bigfoot is real. Even when a Bigfoot was supposedly shot back in 1924, no body or even a drop of blood was ever found. In fact, there has never been any physical evidence, like blood, hair or poo, to prove that Bigfoot exists.

Back in 2014, a team of researchers from Oxford University in the UK tested 36 hair samples that were claimed to belong to Bigfoot or the Yeti (see right). Almost all the hairs turned out to be from animals such as cows, raccoons, deer and humans. But no Bigfoot!

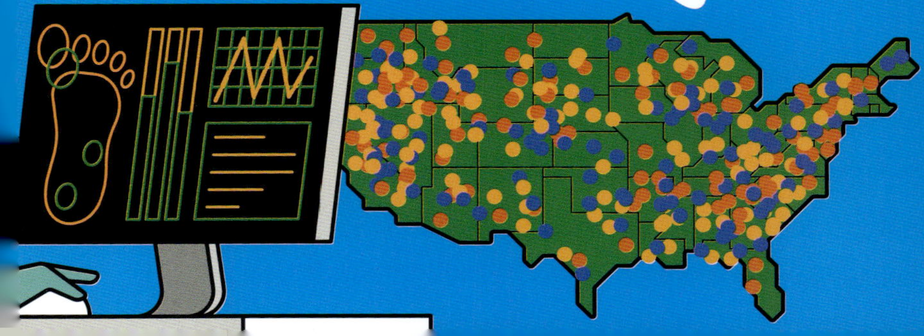

THE YETI

Did you know there are stories of large, hairy, ape-like creatures in many different countries in the world? In the mountains of the Himalayas in Asia there is the Yeti, also known as the Abominable Snowman. Yetis are described very much like Bigfoot – but their fur is white. However, just like Bigfoot, there has been no definitive proof of the Yeti's existence. Well, not *yeti*!

THE MYTH TRUSTER ARGUMENT

Okay Buster, I see your point. But, Chief Detective, let's look at this from another angle . . .

TRUST ARGUMENT ONE:

Why lie?

Yes, eyewitness accounts may not always be accurate, but what did these Bigfoot witnesses get from telling their stories? One line in the Oregon paper in 1924? That's not exactly A-list celebrity status! PLUS, there's evidence from lots of different people at lots of different times reporting the same kinds of sightings. *Coincidence*? Unlikely!

And sightings are still happening today! In October 2023, a couple on a train ride in Colorado, USA noticed a mysterious hairy creature around 2 metres tall squatting in the mountains. It was even recorded on video by another passenger!

A *coincidence* is where similar or related events happen at the same time by chance and without any planning.

TRUST ARGUMENT TWO:

The Bigfoot brains

While the Bigfoot enthusiasts MIGHT be a little biased in their findings, it could also be true that they found the evidence because they knew what to look for. In other words, they were far more likely to find it as they'd done all the research first. In fact, the imprint found in 2000 was only there in the first place because the BFRO researchers had lured the Bigfoot to a muddy spot by leaving fruit there overnight. The next morning, they found the imprint in the mud.

TRUST ARGUMENT THREE:

Camera-shy

While many scientists say the evidence found so far isn't proof, it's also true that no one has yet been able to prove Bigfoot *isn't* real. Many special effects experts who examined the 1967 film footage publicly said at the time that it would be impossible to make such a convincing ape suit with the costumes available in the 1960s.

As for the lack of footage and physical evidence, maybe Bigfoot is simply camera-shy? Maybe Bigfoot wants to avoid the limelight and stop pesky photographers from bothering it! MAYBE Bigfoot doesn't want to be found!

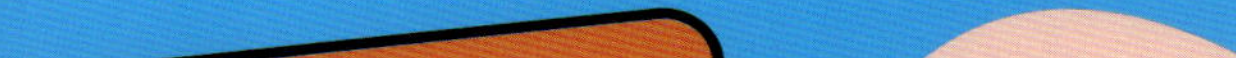

Okay, okay, Truster, it looks like we're not going to agree!

You're right, Buster – something we can agree on! So now we're handing it over to you, Chief Detective.

What do YOU think? Are you a Bigfoot Myth Buster, like me?

Or a Myth Truster, like me?

WHAT DO YOU THINK?

Right, Chief Detective! Let's get to grips with a detective skill that will help to crack open the Bigfoot case. For this mystery, let's explore how to THINK IN GREY.

CRACKING THE CASE

First, read the Detective Skill box on the right. Then, look at the BUST arguments, below, about the Bigfoot evidence and decide how convincing you find them. Imagine a scale from 1–10, where 1 means 'I'm definitely not convinced by this argument' and 10 means 'I'm totally convinced'. What number would you give each argument, and why? Discuss them with a friend or a grown-up.

✦ **You can't always believe eyewitnesses** ✦

✦ **There's never been any physical evidence of Bigfoot** ✦

✦ **The people who claim to have found evidence are biased** ✦

Now SWAP! Look at the TRUST arguments and do the exact same thing. What numbers do you get? Are they higher or lower than your BUST numbers?

✦ **There are SO many similar eyewitness accounts it can't be coincidence** ✦

✦ **There's never been any evidence to say Bigfoot doesn't exist, and maybe Bigfoot just doesn't want to be found** ✦

✦ **Bigfoot researchers find evidence because they're experts who know what they're looking for** ✦

DETECTIVE SKILL

Think in Grey

Have you ever heard the expression 'thinking in black and white'? It means thinking that every question has a simple 'Yes' or 'No' answer. But if you think in grey, it means considering all possibilities and thinking in both 'Yes' *and* 'No'! So, instead of asking yourself, 'Do I believe this, yes or no?', ask yourself '*How confident am I that this is true?*'

Finally ask yourself, in the case of Bigfoot, are you **BUST** or **TRUST**?

BIGFOOT'S DIARY, Summer 1924

Dear Diary,

A very strange thing happened today. We were on a family outing, having a lovely time eating berries and saying hello to elks, when I thought I saw something. It was like a, well, I'm not really sure how to describe it. A sort of hairless ape with little feet.

I moved closer to get a better look and saw there were quite a few of them down by the river. Maybe they were getting rid of their poo. That's where I usually put mine so no one will find it.

I didn't want to disturb them but one of them noticed me. I gave a friendly wave but the silly little creature just ran around in circles shrieking. Then a larger one picked up a funny-looking stick and it let out a loud bang. Steven, ever the clown, decided to pretend he was hit and did a classic pratfall right onto his behind while making a very funny 'ARGHHHHHH' noise. The little feet didn't appreciate it though, as by the time we'd stopped laughing they'd gone. VERY strange.

I do hope they aren't planning to stay long. They're far too noisy for my liking. And they have such odd little feet!

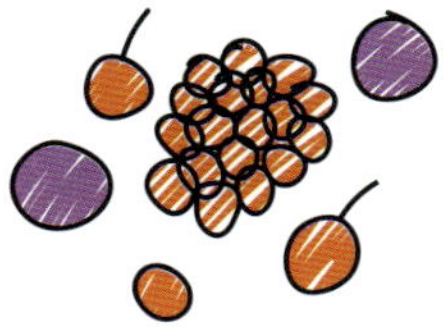

PLACES

THE CURSED TOMBS OF EGYPT

Chief Detective, our next case is a cursed one! Or rather, it's about a curse . . . the cursed tombs of Ancient Egypt to be precise. Now these ancient tombs are pretty, well, ancient, so let's find out a bit of history before we dig into the evidence.

The Ancient Egypt civilization began roughly 5,000 years ago in, you guessed it, Egypt! The Ancient Egyptians are known for many things, including impressive pyramids and a writing system called hieroglyphics (kind of like an alphabet in pictures). But above all else, they are famous for mummies.

Now, you might be thinking, don't most civilizations have mummies? Otherwise who tucks them into bed at night? Well, we're talking about a different kind of mummy! Mummy is the name given to a person or animal who has died but been preserved in some way. The Egyptians made mummies through a complicated process that used a lot of ointments and bandages!

TIMELINE

Pharaoh Tutankhamun is buried.

1324 BCE

Howard Carter and a team of archaeologists open King Tutankhamun's tomb.

1922

George Jay Gould visits the tomb and dies almost immediately after.

1923

Life After Death

Preserving the bodies of the dead might seem a little gross to us, but the Ancient Egyptians had a reason for it. They believed in an afterlife, where a person could live for eternity if they were judged to be worthy. The person who had died needed their body in the afterlife, as it was the home of their spirit, or soul. That is why dead bodies were mummified, to preserve them.

The Ancient Egyptians also believed they could take their belongings with them to the afterlife. So rich citizens and pharaohs, who were the kings and queens of Egypt, were buried in large tombs with lots of valuable things, including fancy clothes, statues, jewellery and even their favourite animals! Some big, impressive tombs had threats written on them to warn people they shouldn't try to steal any of the treasures.

Curse or Coincidence?

Over the years, many people have discovered tombs buried under the sands of Egypt. Some people went looking for them for research, and unfortunately others just wanted to pocket the amazing treasures. BUT many of those who dared to enter the pharaohs' tombs have suffered strange illnesses and terrible accidents. This had led some people to claim they are cursed . . .

But we're getting ahead of ourselves. Come on, Chief Detective, let's have a look at the evidence and then you can decide if you TRUST or BUST the cursed tombs of Egypt!

Howard Carter gives Bruce Ingham the ghoulish gift of a mummy's hand!
1925
R.I.P.
Richard Bethell, who entered the tomb with Howard Carter, is killed.
1929
Tutankhamun's treasures are moved and another spooky death occurs!
1972

Turn the page to keep reading and find out about these events, and more!

THE EVIDENCE

Okay, Chief Detective, here are three pieces of evidence that will help you decide whether you're an ancient curse Buster or Truster.

FIRST PIECE OF EVIDENCE:

Tomb curses

Before we start, it's worth mentioning that many tombs have been discovered in Ancient Egypt, but hardly any have warnings or threats written on them. However, some definitely do, and some of these curses are pretty scary!

For example, in 1990 the famous Egyptian archaeologist Zahi Hawass discovered a curse at the tombs of the pyramids at Giza. According to him, it said: 'All people who enter this tomb who will make evil against this tomb and destroy it, may the crocodile be against them in water, and snakes against them on land. May the hippopotamus be against them in water, the scorpion on land.'

Now that's a pretty scary curse if ever there was one! After reading it, Zahi Hawass decided not to disturb the mummies.

SECOND PIECE OF EVIDENCE:

The opening of Tutankhamun's tomb, 1922

When Tutankhamun's tomb was discovered in 1922, it was BIG news. Tutankhamun was not an especially famous pharaoh, but his tomb had been pretty well protected from robbers, so there was still lots of treasure inside. The dig was paid for by a man named Lord Carnarvon, and led by British archaeologist Howard Carter.

It wasn't long before people involved in the dig started dying under quite mysterious circumstances. Lord Carnarvon was the first. He died just five months after the tomb was discovered. And then the deaths kept happening! American businessman George Jay Gould died almost straight after visiting the tomb in 1923, and in 1929 Richard Bethell, one of the first people to enter the tomb behind Howard Carter, was killed.

What's strange though, is that Howard Carter, the man who led the expedition, *didn't* die suddenly or mysteriously. In fact, he lived for nearly 20 more years. Maybe the curse made a mistake?

THIRD PIECE OF EVIDENCE:

Gift of a mummy's hand, 1925(ish)

The final piece of evidence is a ghoulish gift that Howard Carter gave his friend, Sir Bruce Ingham, in 1925 (or thereabouts). The gift was a mummy's hand wearing a bracelet with these words written on it: 'Cursed be he who moves my body, they that shall break the seal of this tomb shall meet death by a disease that no doctor can diagnose . . .'

Creepy! Apparently Howard Carter thought his friend could use the hand as a paperweight. What a truly terrible gift! Soon after, Sir Bruce's house burnt down, and when he tried to rebuild it, it was destroyed again in a flood. That seems like definitive proof of a mummy's curse in action!

HOWEVER, it's worth remembering that it was Howard Carter who actually disturbed the mummy, not Sir Bruce. If the curse was real, shouldn't it have been Howard Carter who suffered the consequences?

Okay, Chief Detective! Let's dust off the evidence and prove that the idea of cursed tombs is all a bit far-fetched (or should I say *pharaoh*-fetched?)

THE MYTH BUSTER ARGUMENT

BUST ARGUMENT ONE:

To curse or not to curse!

The first piece of evidence stated that the Egyptian archaeologist Zahi Hawass was scared off by the curses written on the pyramids in Giza. However, this doesn't mean the curses were real. It could simply be that Hawass had a guilty conscience. A *conscience* means knowing right from wrong. Many people have questioned whether it's right to disturb Egypt's mummies. After all, the Ancient Egyptian people believed they needed their bodies for the afterlife, and we should respect their beliefs.

In fact, Zahi Hawass himself felt that the way mummies used to be displayed in museums was not very respectful, and he has since made sure that it is done in a much nicer way in Egypt.

BUST ARGUMENT TWO:

Deadly disasters & lone survivors

Yes, it's true that a lot of people involved in the Tutankhamun dig died. But many of them actually died from unfortunate yet perfectly normal causes!

One of the most famous deaths was that of Lord Carnarvon, who died shortly after opening the tomb. HOWEVER, he actually died of an infected mosquito bite. Back then, people didn't know as much about infections as we do now. So Lord Carnarvon's death seemed a lot more mysterious at the time than it really was!

And then there's Howard Carter. He was the leader of the expedition and arguably the person who treated the mummy with the most disrespect. Let's not forget that he once gave a mummy's hand as a present! Howard Carter didn't believe in the curses – he called them 'tommy-rot'. And maybe he was right. After all, Howard Carter lived to the age of 64, which was a pretty long life back in the 1930s!

BUST ARGUMENT THREE:

Bad news, big headlines!

There were rumours about cursed Egyptian tombs even before Carter's team dug up Tutankhamun's tomb, but there's no doubt that Lord Carnavon's death fanned the flames of the legend – and soon 'King Tut's Curse' was all the newspapers could write about! It wasn't long before *any* misfortune was seen as proof of the curse's power. For example, in 1970 an expedition member's traffic accident was linked to the curse by the *London Times* newspaper – even though it was a whole 48 years later!

Here's the BIG point though – there wasn't even a curse written on Tutankhamun's tomb! Or at least, no curses were ever found. So, how can people die of a curse that doesn't exist? This didn't stop the newspapers writing about 'King Tut's Curse' of course – nothing gets in the way of a good story!

THE MYTH TRUSTER ARGUMENT

Okay, Chief Detective! Let's unwrap more of this mystery and present the Truster side of the argument. I'll convince you that the tombs really were cursed!

TRUST ARGUMENT ONE:

The Valley of the Golden Mummies

The Egyptian archaeologist Zahi Hawass is something of an expert when it comes to Egyptian history. You've already read how he decided to leave the tombs in Giza alone, but did you know he also claims to have been cursed himself? Well, kind of . . .

In 1996, he discovered the Valley of the Golden Mummies, a huge burial site containing thousands of mummies. When two child mummies were moved from the valley to a museum, Hawass claimed to be haunted by the mummy children in his dreams. According to him, the nightmares only stopped when the mummy father was reunited with the mummy children in the museum!

It's fair to say that Hawass might not be a reliable witness when it comes to curses, since his beliefs about them keep changing. However, it is clear that he believes the mummies should be respected and treated with care.

TRUST ARGUMENT TWO:

The case of Carter's canary

It's true that nothing bad happened *directly* to Howard Carter, but there's no denying that lots of bad things happened *around* him.

Take, for instance, the case of Carter's pet canary. One day, shortly after the tomb was opened, Carter's pet bird was discovered in the mouth of a cobra, which had seemingly appeared from nowhere. Now, can you guess which animal was carved on two statues of Tutankhamun found in his tomb? That's right, cobras! Carter's Egyptian staff saw this spooky incident as a warning from Tutankhamun's spirit.

It has been claimed that the incident was an act of protest by some local gangs who didn't like Tutankhamun's tomb being disturbed. But if the cobra was put there by people, they were never found. Either way, poor canary!

TRUST ARGUMENT THREE:

Coincidences or curses?

While it's true that not everyone involved in the dig died, it's also true that there is a repeating pattern of strange things happening to people who get involved with Tutankhamun's treasure.

For instance, Dr Gamal Mehrez of the British Museum is rumoured to have laughed at the curses when he was in charge of moving the tomb's treasures to London in 1972. This was long after the tomb was originally opened. And yet, Dr Mehrez died the night after overseeing the cargo's transportation . . . Scary!

So Chief Detective, it's time to decide . . .

Are you a Truster in the cursed tombs of Ancient Egypt? Like me!

Or do you think it's all just tommy-rot? Like me!

WHAT DO YOU THINK?

Okay, Chief Detective, let's dig some more and uncover some new detective skills! For this mystery, let's look at how to DO INDEPENDENT RESEARCH.

CRACKING THE CASE

You've read and considered the evidence in this book, but now it's time for you to do some research of your own! With a grown-up, see what evidence YOU can find that supports or challenges the myth of the cursed tombs. You could read books or search the internet for articles, videos and podcasts.

Now, for the fun bit! Grab a pen and paper and draw or write down any evidence you find in two columns – one for Bust and one for Trust. Which column has the most convincing evidence in it?

Now, ask yourself, are you **BUSTING** or **TRUSTING** this mystery?

DETECTIVE SKILL

Do Independent Research

Here are some tips for how to find reliable information:

1. **Use Reliable Sources:** Look for information from trustworthy sources, such as books from school libraries, or the websites of governments or news organizations. Be cautious of information on social media as it might be biased or false.

2. **Cross-check Information**: Remember to compare the information you find against other sources. If different sources show the same information, they're more likely to be reliable. If they contradict each other, you should investigate further!

3. **Be Critical:** Question the evidence! Ask questions such as: Who created this content? What evidence supports their claims?

BUST! TRUST
Happy birthday Bruce, old chum!
Er . . . no, no, it's definitely not my birthday, Howard.
Then why do you have a birthday cake and a big banner saying 'Happy Birthday'?
HAPPY BIRTHD
Er, okay, today is my birthday, but . . . Don't take this the wrong way, Howard, but every time you give me a gift it causes awful bad luck!
Remember when you gave me that mask? My dear dog Cedric Woofington mysteriously disappeared and I swear I heard that mask burping . . .
BUUUUURRRP
Coincidence! Sadly pets do just run off sometimes, Bruce.
Or when you gave me that monkey's paw to use as a bookmark? And then a plague of locusts ate my curtains!
Well, I'll admit that WAS unfortunate. But this time I promise I've got you a gift with no curses!
Isn't it glorious? The perfect paperweight, wouldn't you say?
Oh, a mummified hand! How, er, unusual . . .
Do you smell burning? Howard? Howard? HOWAAARRRDDD!!!
HAPP
TRUST ! BUST

THE CURIOUS CASE OF AMELIA EARHART

Chief Detectives, fasten your seatbelts, because this next case is very famous! You are going to investigate the mystery of Amelia Earhart, the pilot whose aeroplane suddenly disappeared. Are you ready for take-off? Here we go!

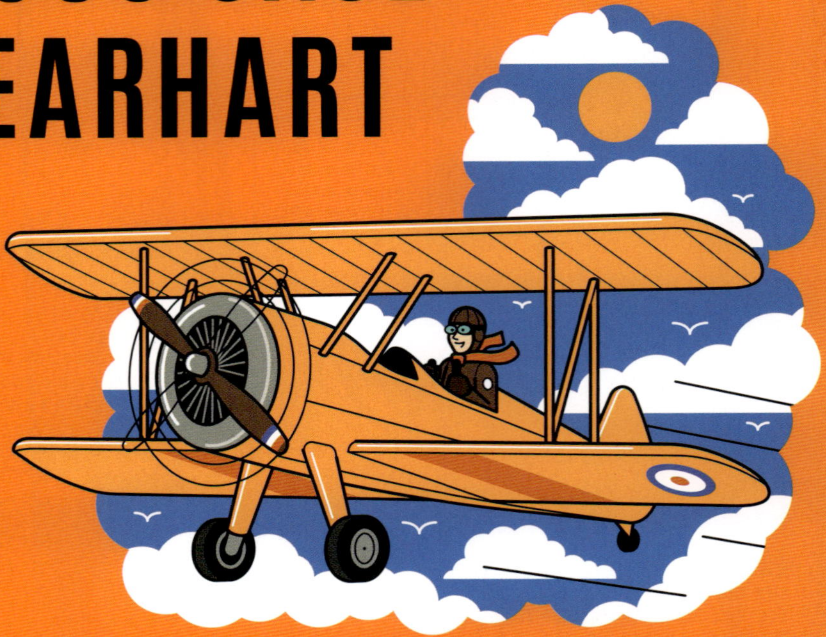

Amelia Earhart was an extraordinary American pilot who set many world records. In 1932, she became the first woman to fly by herself across the Atlantic Ocean. This was an amazing achievement because when Amelia was flying, planes were very different to today. They were smaller, they had no computers to help with navigation, and they were nowhere near as safe – flying used to be quite a risky thing to do back then. But that didn't put off adventurous Amelia! She was very passionate about flying and did a lot to encourage more women to fly too. In her lifetime, she won the Distinguished Flying Cross and the Légion d'honneur, as well as earning a place in America's National Aviation Hall of Fame and the National Women's Hall of Fame.

TIMELINE

1937 – Amelia and Fred disappear over the Pacific. Eyewitnesses claim to have seen the plane land safely, and there are reports of distress calls.

1939 – After two years of searching, Amelia and Fred are declared dead.

1940 – Bones are found alongside a navigation tool on Nikumaroro Island.

A Vanishing Act

In 1937, Amelia and her trusty navigator Fred Noonan set off to fly all the way around the world. Back then, planes could only carry a small amount of fuel, so needed to stop a lot – the trip was planned to take about 30 days. On 2 July 1937, Amelia, Fred and the plane were flying over the Pacific Ocean heading towards tiny Howland Island, when Amelia radioed to say they were running low on fuel. Soon after that, the plane completely disappeared and they were never seen again.

Water, Water Everywhere

The Pacific is the largest and deepest of the oceans on Earth. There are some small island nations scattered throughout it, like Fiji, Samoa and the Marshall Islands, but for thousands of miles there is nothing but water. It's a pretty big area to go looking for someone who has disappeared, and so to this day, no one knows exactly what happened to Amelia and Fred. Did they manage to land safely on an island, or did they lose their lives when their plane ran out of fuel and crashed into the ocean?

So now it's up to you, our Chief Detective, to decide if you TRUST or BUST that Amelia Earhart somehow survived in 1937.

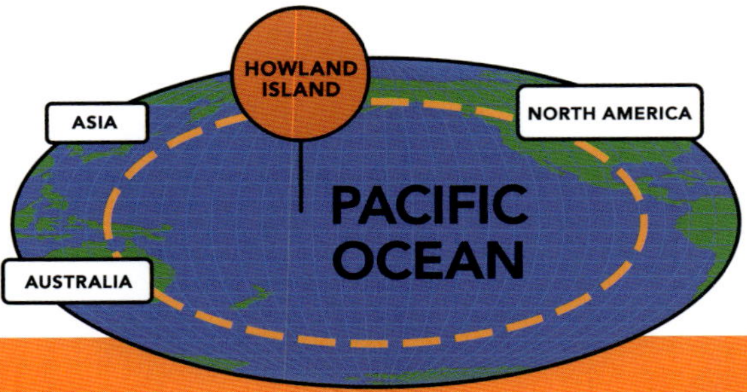

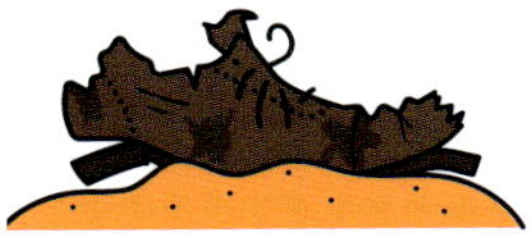

The remains of a shoe are found on Nikumaroro.

1991

New forensic tests are done based on the measurements of the bones.

2018

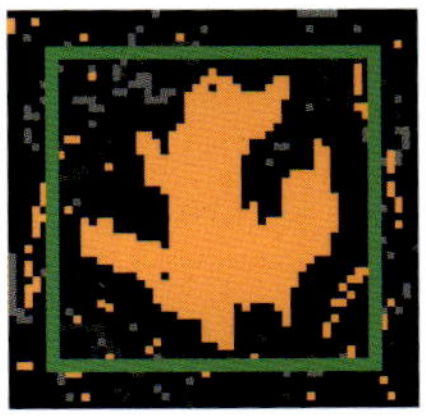

Images of a plane are captured in the Pacific Ocean.

2024

Turn the page to keep reading and find out about these events, and more!

THE EVIDENCE

Okay, Chief Detective, the evidence we're about to show you will help you decide where you think Amelia Earhart might have ended up. With each piece of evidence, you decide whether you're going to Bust or Trust the *theory* that she survived.

FIRST PIECE OF EVIDENCE:

Eyewitness account, summer 1937

A *theory* is an idea or set of ideas that is intended to explain facts or events.

I saw Amelia Earhart land on Saipan in the summer of 1937 . . . [Soldiers] surrounded the plane and, a little later, escorted two people past me: a fairly tall slim woman with a short haircut and dressed in man's clothing; and a tall man who was wearing dark trousers and a light shirt with short sleeves.

Josephine Blanco Akiyama

After Amelia's disappearance in 1937, lots of people claimed to have seen her land the plane safely. One of the most famous eyewitness accounts comes from Josephine Blanco Akiyama, who was born and raised on a Pacific island called Saipan, which at the time was occupied by the Japanese army. She claimed that Amelia and Fred were taken prisoner, which might explain why they didn't contact anyone to let them know they were OK. And Josephine wasn't the only eyewitness on Saipan.

However, there are also eyewitness accounts of Amelia's plane supposedly landing on *different* Pacific islands. She can't have landed on all of them at the same time!

SECOND PIECE OF EVIDENCE:

Distress calls, summer 1937

The second piece of evidence are the distress calls that were heard by many different witnesses across the Pacific. A distress call is a signal sent, usually by radio, from a plane or a boat that is in danger.

These distress calls suggest Amelia landed safely, but unfortunately they're not quite proof. The days that followed her disappearance were very confusing, because there were lots of *hoax* claims from people saying they had picked up signals from the missing pair.

It is possible though that Amelia's genuine signals simply got lost amongst all the hoaxes. Ric Gillespie, the founder of the International Group of Historic Aviation Recovery, analysed over 100 distress signals that were reported in the six days after she vanished. He concluded that 57 of them were believable. Maybe he is right?

Detective, do you remember what a *hoax* means? Check your Detective Dictionary!

THIRD PIECE OF EVIDENCE:

Bones discovered in 1940 and shoe found in 1991

In 1940, human bones were found on the uninhabited Pacific island of Nikumaroro, next to a bottle and a navigational tool called a sextant. A doctor in Fiji who examined the bones at the time said they were likely those of a European man. Fred Noonan was American – perhaps the bones could have been his?

Then, in 1991, a team that included Ric Gillespie landed on Nikumaroro and found the remains of a shoe. It was made in the 1930s and looked similar to a pair that Earhart was photographed wearing days before she disappeared. If it was Amelia's, maybe this is proof that she was a castaway on the island?

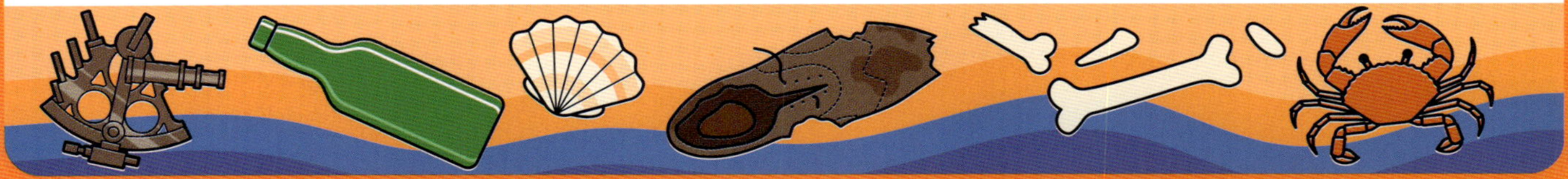

Okay, Chief Detective! Let's Bust the evidence and prove that Amelia and Fred crashed into the ocean and sadly did not survive.

THE MYTH BUSTER ARGUMENT

BUST ARGUMENT ONE:

Amelia everywhere (and nowhere?)

As you read earlier, eyewitnesses on different islands all claimed to have seen Amelia and Fred land their plane. As well as the accounts from Saipan, there were also reports of Amelia landing in the Marshall Islands – in fact the people there were so convinced this happened that they made special stamps to remember it! But these supposed eyewitnesses can't *all* be right.

What's more, if Amelia and Fred did land safely, why were they never found? Franklin D. Roosevelt, the American president at the time, led a massive two-week search for the pair, and Amelia's husband, George Putnam, paid for his own private searches after the government stopped looking. But the searches turned up nothing.

One theory was that Amelia was captured by the Japanese army. Some people even thought that she became a Japanese spy! The problem with these theories is that there is no evidence for them. They are only *hearsay*.

Hearsay is information that you hear but do not know to be true.

BUST ARGUMENT TWO:

Bone idle

Next, let's look at the bones and the items found next to them in Nikumaroro. Unfortunately, the bones themselves were lost long ago, so there's no way to have them tested again. Without DNA testing of the bones, we'll never know for certain who they belonged to.

And then there's the mysterious Nikumaroro shoe. The shoe did look very similar to a pair Amelia wore. However, it was a size 9 – which some experts argue would have been too big for Earhart. So, once again, it's not solid proof!

Finally, if Amelia and Fred DID land safely on Nikumaroro, why has their plane not been found there?

BUST ARGUMENT THREE:

The evidence is plane

In January 2024, deep-sea explorer brothers Tony and Lloyd Romeo announced that they may have found something exciting at the bottom of the ocean – the long-lost plane of Amelia Earhart!

A crew of 16 researchers and operators scanned over 5,200 square miles of the Pacific Ocean using sonar imaging, which uses sound waves to map the ocean floor. They captured images of a plane-shaped object lying on the ocean floor, less than 100 miles from Howland Island, which is where Amelia and Fred were supposed to land. The team believe the plane might have run out of fuel and crash-landed in the sea.

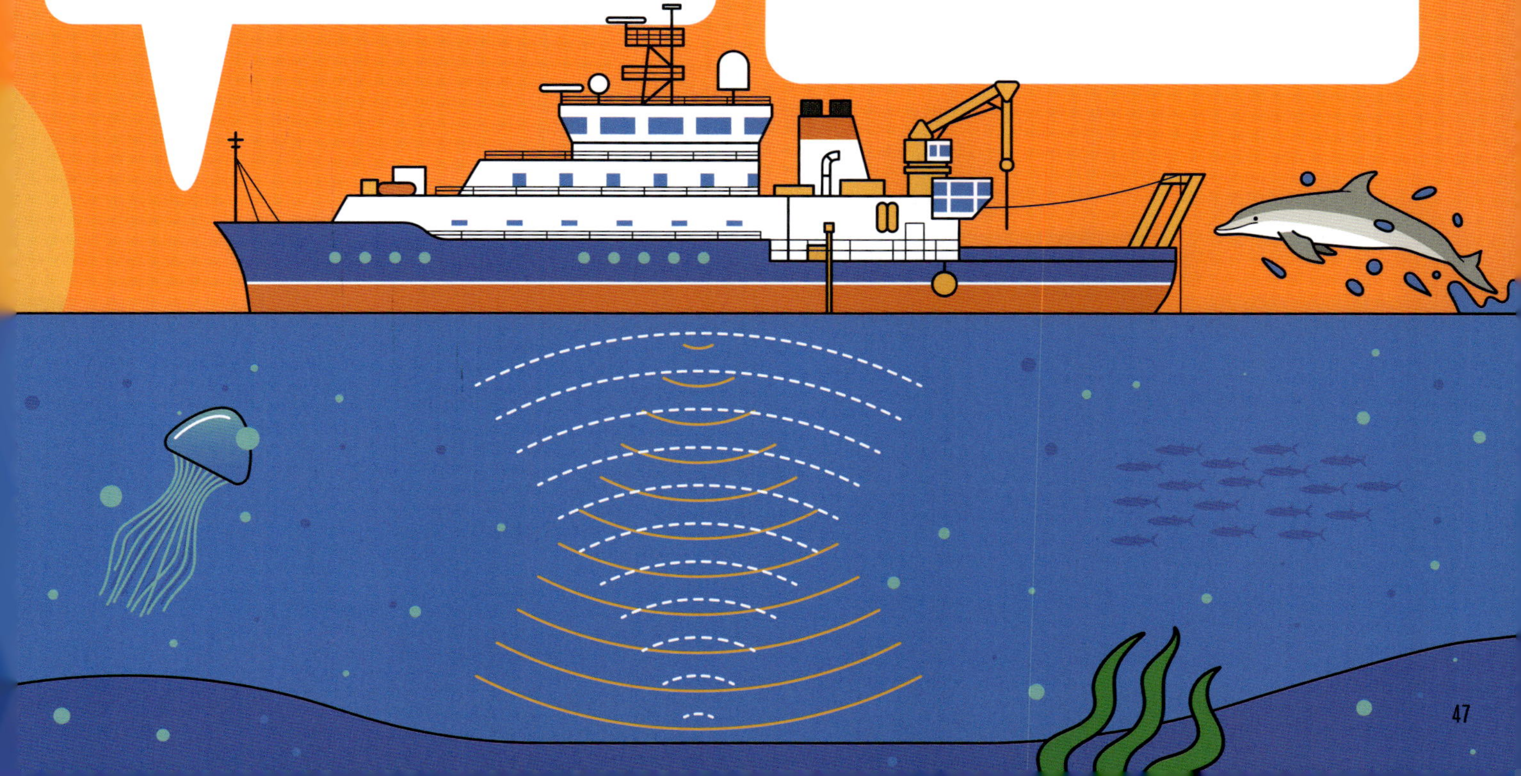

THE MYTH TRUSTER ARGUMENT

Okay Buster, you've made some good arguments there. But let's look at the Trust side of things, and I'll try to prove that Amelia and Fred landed safely.

TRUST ARGUMENT ONE:

To be Pacific!

Chief Detective, did you know that there are over 25,000 islands in the Pacific Ocean?! People only live on a few of them though, and that's because many of them are tiny and very far apart, making it too hard for anyone to settle there. Despite the many different searches for Amelia, there's no way that every single island was searched from top to bottom. So it's very possible that Amelia and Fred ended up on one of them.

TRUST ARGUMENT TWO:

Shipwrecked

It turns out, when the bones found on Nikumaroro Island were first examined in 1940, lots of errors were made. In 2018, a scientist used modern forensic tests to compare the size of the bones recorded by the doctor in 1940, to what they thought Amelia's bone lengths were, based on her clothing and photographs. The study found that not only are the bones female, but they are also more similar to Amelia's bones than 99 per cent of people they used as a sample!

Now, remember the other items found on the island – the sextant, the bottle and the shoe? If you put all the evidence together, it starts to look very likely that Amelia was shipwrecked on Nikumaroro Island.

TRUST ARGUMENT THREE:

Plainly not Amelia's plane

Let's take another look at that sonar image from 2024. The team that took it believe it could show Amelia's plane, but many other experts are not so sure. Ric Gillespie (remember him?) thinks the image is unclear, and argues that even if it is a plane, its wings don't match those of the plane Amelia flew.

Plus, if the skeleton on Nikumaroro Island *is* Amelia Earhart, then the plane under the sea definitely can't be hers, as the two sites are too far away from each other.

So, Chief Detective, there you have it! All the evidence is in front of you.

Of course, more evidence might appear one day. And if it does, it's important to remember that you can always change your mind.

Busters can always become Trusters!

And Trusters can become Busters!

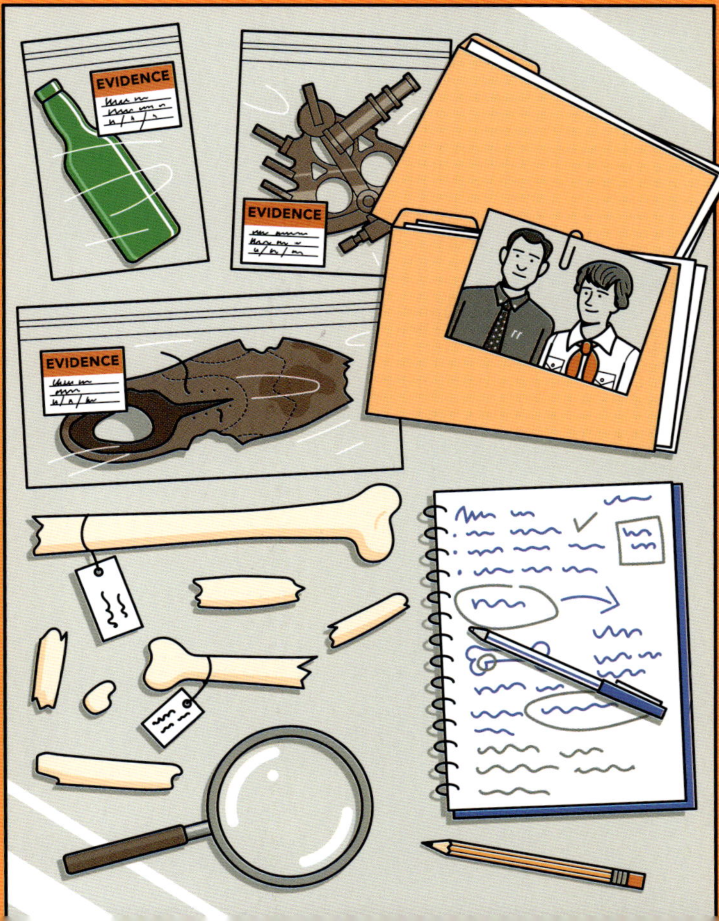

WHAT DO YOU THINK?

Okay, Chief Detective! It's time for you to Bust or Trust the theory that Amelia survived after her plane mysteriously disappeared. Let's crack open the case using a new detective skill. Let's . . . EVALUATE TESTIMONY!

CRACKING THE CASE

First read the Detective Skill box on the right. The case of Amelia Earhart is filled with lots of different testimonies, from eyewitnesses claiming to have seen Amelia, to experts who have different opinions on planes and bones. All of which makes this case especially difficult!

Look at the list of testimonies below. Can you decide which type each one is: eyewitness, hearsay or expert opinion?

- **Claims are made that Amelia is a Japanese spy**
- **Distress calls are heard in the summer of 1937**
- **Doctor in Fiji says bones found are from a man, 1940**
- **Josephine Bianco Akiyama claims to have seen Amelia in Saipan, 1937**

Once you've done that, you can decide how RELIABLE these testimonies are and whether or not you are Busting or Trusting them!

Finally, do you **TRUST** that Amelia Earhart survived or are you a **BUSTER** who thinks she died when her plane crashed into the sea?

DETECTIVE SKILL
Evaluate Testimony

Some different types of testimony:

1. **Eyewitness:** This is where someone claims to have seen an event in person.

2. **Hearsay**: This is where someone has heard something from someone else and reports it.

3. **Expert opinion**: This is where an expert provides an opinion about something based on the evidence in front of them.

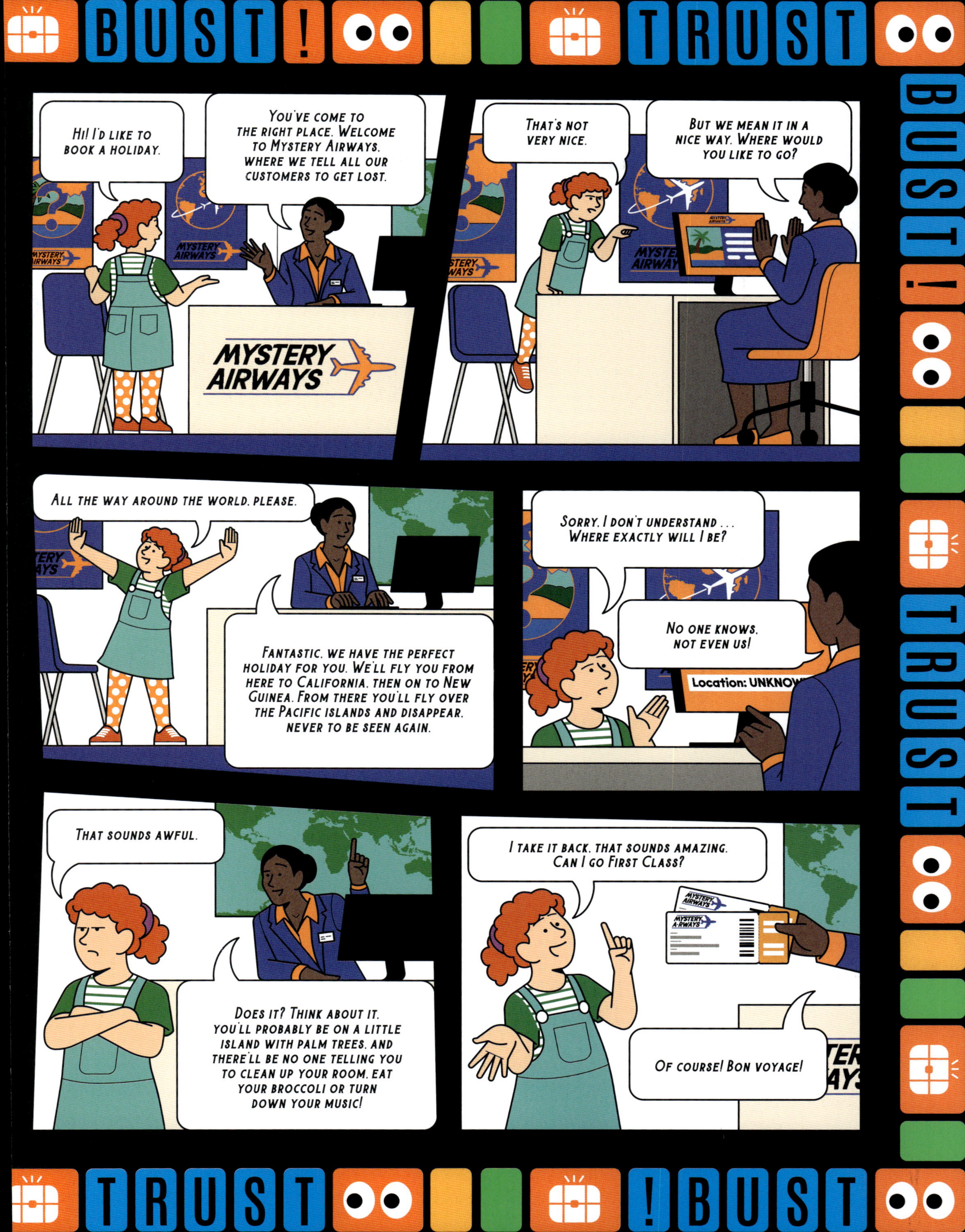
BUST! TRUST
BUST! TRUST
Hi! I'd like to book a holiday.
You've come to the right place. Welcome to Mystery Airways, where we tell all our customers to get lost.
MYSTERY AIRWAYS
That's not very nice.
But we mean it in a nice way. Where would you like to go?
All the way around the world, please.
Fantastic, we have the perfect holiday for you. We'll fly you from here to California, then on to New Guinea. From there you'll fly over the Pacific islands and disappear, never to be seen again.
Sorry, I don't understand . . . Where exactly will I be?
No one knows, not even us!
Location: UNKNOW
That sounds awful.
Does it? Think about it. You'll probably be on a little island with palm trees, and there'll be no one telling you to clean up your room, eat your broccoli or turn down your music!
I take it back, that sounds amazing. Can I go First Class?
Of course! Bon voyage!
TRUST ! BUST

OKIKU THE HAUNTED DOLL

Okay, Myth Busters and Trusters! Our next case is a bit of a hair-raising one. Or at least, a hair-growing one! It's all about the mystery of Okiku, the haunted, hair-growing doll from Hokkaido in Japan.

Japan is a country on the eastern edge of Asia – in fact, it is known as the 'Land of the Rising Sun', because the Sun rises in the east. It is made up of five main islands, called Hokkaido, Honshu, Shikoku, Kyushu and Okinawa, as well as many smaller ones. The main religions of Japan are Shinto and Buddhism, but many people practise both. The country is also famous for delicious food like sushi and ramen noodles.

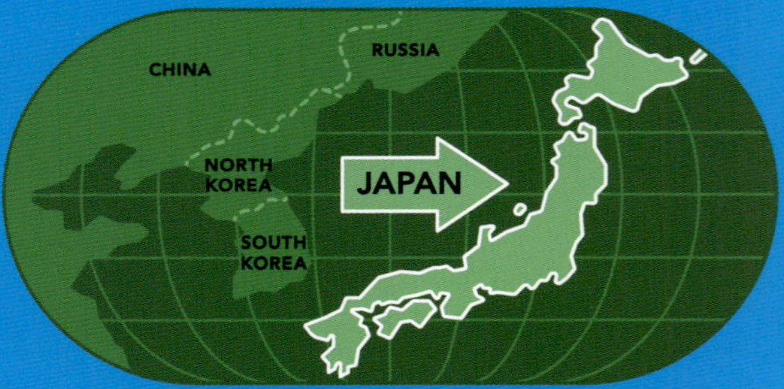

→ TIMELINE →

Earliest record of Japanese hōko dolls being made using human hair.

1333

A girl named Okiku is given a doll by her brother and names it after herself.

1918

The little girl Okiku sadly passes away.

1919

Okiku's Tale

The story of Okiku the haunted doll goes back to 1918, when a teenage boy named Eikichi Suzuki bought a large doll for his younger sister, Okiku. Okiku and the doll became inseparable, and she even named it after herself. But tragedy struck a year later, when the little girl died.

Soon afterwards, her family noticed that the hair on the doll was growing! They came to believe that Okiku's spirit was inhabiting the doll. The story of Okiku is now so famous it's become a popular tale in Japanese *folklore*.

In Japanese, the name Okiku means 'chrysanthemum', a pretty flower that is native to East Asia.

Folklore is the term used to describe collections of stories and beliefs from communities around the world.

Okiku's Temple

Okiku the haunted doll currently resides in the Mannenji Temple on Hokkaido island, where she has her own private shrine. The priests there supposedly trim Okiku's still-growing hair! Apparently the doll visits the priests' dreams, as well as the dreams of those that come to visit her. Another rumour is that Okiku's mouth is slowly opening and that if you dare to peer inside you may be able to glimpse something like baby teeth . . . So, if you're ever in Japan, she might be worth a visit!

Okay, Chief Detective, are you ready to hear more about the doll who grows hair . . . or rather, are you ready to decide IF the doll grows hair? Let's Bust or Trust this haunted tale!

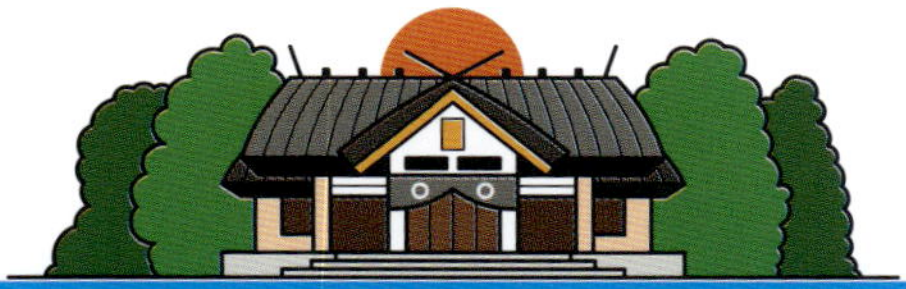

The doll is moved to a temple to be looked after by priests.

1938

Photos taken by the priests show Okiku with long hair.

Date unknown

A hair sample from Okiku is tested.

Date unknown

Turn the page to keep reading and find out about these events, and more!

THE EVIDENCE

Okay, Chief Detective! Let's take a look at the evidence and then you can decide if Okiku really does grow her own hair, Rapunzel-style!

FIRST PIECE OF EVIDENCE:

Testimony of Okiku's family

Piece of evidence number one (or number *ichi* as they say in Japanese!) is the testimony of the family themselves.

After Okiku sadly passed away, her family placed Okiku's doll on their altar to remember her. As Japan is a Shinto and Buddhist country, it's very common to have a small shrine or altar in the house. This either looks like a very small temple if it's Shinto, or a small wooden cabinet if it's Buddhist. These altars are usually a place for praying and remembering lost family and ancestors.

Soon after Okiku passed, the family started noticing something very strange about the doll. When Okiku was alive, the doll had what is called an *okappa* hairstyle – so her hair was shoulder-length and very straight, with a straight fringe or 'bangs'. But after Okiku's death, the doll's hair began to grow. Other unusual things also began happening in the house, like noises, banging and lights flickering. The family soon became convinced the doll was haunted and that this explained the growing hair.

However, they didn't keep any evidence of these strange and sinister happenings – no written accounts, no photos, no video or sound recordings, nothing!

SECOND PIECE OF EVIDENCE:

Photographs of Okiku

Pieces of evidence number two (or number *ni*!) are photographs of Okiku. As we mentioned earlier, the doll has been staying at a temple in Hokkaido since 1938. The priests allow visitors to go and see her, but they don't allow photos. So the only photos we have come from the priests themselves, which tend to be a little blurry. Maybe the priests have got other things to do rather than try and work out what setting works best on a camera?

Quality of the pictures aside, the photos clearly show a doll with long, straggly hair – certainly NOT the straight, shoulder-length hair the doll used to have. The priests have agreed that the doll's hair grows, and they have been giving her haircuts ever since she came to the temple!

THIRD PIECE OF EVIDENCE:

Tests on the doll's hair

Piece of evidence number three (or number *san*) is the fact that the priests supposedly had one of the doll's hairs tested, and the results confirmed that it was human hair!

What does this mean? Well, on the one hand it COULD show that when the doll was taken over by the girl's spirit, its hair became human, and that's why it keeps getting longer . . .

OR, maybe it doesn't actually prove anything at all. In 1918, most dolls had human hair. Japanese hōko dolls can be traced back to the 14th century, and were traditionally made of silk and human hair, and stuffed with cotton. In fact, plastic doll hair wasn't used much until after 1945.

Okay, Chief Detective, let's *untangle* this mystery and BUST this case!

THE MYTH BUSTER ARGUMENT

BUST ARGUMENT ONE:

Phone-y stories

It's always good to have an eyewitness when weighing evidence. However, the eyewitness accounts of Okiku's family might not be that reliable. Remember, the family had been through a lot. Having lost Okiku at a young age, they might have simply been seeing what they *wanted* to see.

It's also possible that the story of Okiku the doll has been *exaggerated* over the years as it has been told and re-told. Tales and stories often change shape over time. Have you heard of the Phone Game? It's a popular game in which a message is whispered from person to person until it reaches the last player. When the original message and the final message are compared, more often than not they are completely different! It's a fun game, but also shows how easily a story can change when passed from person to person. Something similar might well have happened with the story of Okiku.

To *exaggerate* means to present something as bigger or more important than it is.

BUST ARGUMENT TWO:

Splitting hairs

As mentioned before, Okiku having human hair isn't quite as strange as it might sound, because real human hair was often used to make dolls in the days before plastic became common. The hair in these old dolls was often attached by knots inside the head. And get this – over time, the threads holding these knots together can start to fall apart, allowing strands of hair to slip out, making the hair look longer!

So, maybe the explanation for Okiku's hair 'growing' is just that it started to untie? After all, she is a really old doll now and this would definitely explain some of her mysterious hair growth.

BUST ARGUMENT THREE:

Dolled-up!

Did you know that dolls are an important part of Japanese culture? There are several traditional dolls in different styles, and even festivals for dolls. The most popular type of dolls are Ningyo, which look like humans and are often very beautiful – almost like works of art. In many countries, the word 'doll' refers to toy dolls. But in Japan, there is still a strong idea that anything made into the shape of living creatures is special, and sometimes dolls are treated as if they are alive.

Dolls feature in many Japanese myths and legends too. Given all this, doesn't it seem likely that Okiku is just another legendary doll to add to the list of Japanese myths?

THE MYTH TRUSTER ARGUMENT

Okay, Chief Detective, let me present some arguments why you should TRUST that Okiku really is a haunted, hair-growing doll!

TRUST ARGUMENT ONE:

Haunted houses

Okiku's family might not be the most reliable eyewitnesses, but they aren't the only ones who claim that Okiku is a haunted doll. When the family first *suspected* the doll was haunted, they brought in all sorts of spiritual leaders to examine it, and they all said the same thing: that the soul of the little girl Okiku was trapped within the doll.

By 1938, the family had grown quite attached to the haunted doll and their daughter's restless spirit. They wanted to move house but feared taking the doll with them – they were worried its magic might stop working if it was moved too far away from their daughter's grave. That's why Okiku was moved to a nearby temple and into the priests' care.

From family to priests to tourists, there are people all over the world who believe Okiku is a doll with a human spirit! Why would they all believe it, if it weren't a little bit true?

Suspected means to have an idea about something or to believe something could be true.

TRUST ARGUMENT TWO:

No hair out of place!

Okay, I admit, Buster has given some reasons that could explain why Okiku had human hair AND how strands of it might have got longer when they became detached. But even if Buster is right, that doesn't explain why Okiku's hair KEEPS growing! Originally the doll had a traditional shoulder-length cut with neat ends, but over time this grew into a long mess of split-ends. The family said that the new hair was a different colour to the doll's original hair, and that it felt different too.

Photos of Okiku clearly show a doll with long, straggly hair down to her knees. And that's with the priests regularly cutting it! Imagine how long her hair would be if they weren't giving her a good trim from time to time?

TRUST ARGUMENT THREE:

Tiny teeth

Finally, let's not forget the reports from some visitors to the temple that Okiku's mouth is beginning to open and she is starting to grow teeth. It appears that she really is turning into a human. Soon the priests will have to start brushing her teeth as well as her hair!

Sadly, there aren't any photos of Okiku's new teeth. Apparently the doll has told the priests that she doesn't want to have any photos taken, and that is why there aren't any recent images of her. See what happens? She gets all famous with the hair trick and then acts like a celebrity – no pics please, tell the paparazzi to leave!

So now we're handing it over to you, Chief Detective!

What do YOU think?

Are you a Buster who thinks this case is as fake as a plastic doll?

Or are you a Truster who thinks Okiku's hair really is growing?

WHAT DO YOU THINK?

Right, Chief Detective, there's no more time to split hairs! To solve this case, let's look at a new detective skill – CHECK FOR PERSONAL BIAS.

CRACKING THE CASE

First, read the Detective Skill box on the right. Then take a look at this list of people involved in the case of Okiku the Haunted Doll:

- **Okiku's family**
- **Priests**
- **Tourists**

On a piece of paper write out any reasons why each of these groups of people might WANT Okiku to be haunted. Give yourself some time to consider your answers – are any of these reasons motivated by personal bias?

Now, on another piece of paper, write out any reasons why each of these groups of people might NOT want Okiku to be haunted.

Now decide, are you **BUSTING** or **TRUSTING** Okiku the Haunted Doll?

DETECTIVE SKILL

Check for Personal Bias

Imagine you have a favourite footballer – let's call them Steven. You find Steven really inspiring, but one day, there's a story in the newspaper about him. It says he is rude to his fans and shouts at his teammates. Because you admire Steven so much, you might ignore the story or make excuses for his behaviour, despite the evidence that he is not such an amazing person after all.

This is called 'bias' or 'motivated reasoning' – it's when what we want to believe influences what we do believe. Sometimes it's hard to overcome our bias, even in the face of evidence!

OKIKU'S DIARY, 1 July

Dear Diary,

Having this amazing, long, beautiful hair is hard work. Really and truly it is. In fact, people from all over the world come to see me and my lovely long hair. For a doll, I'm basically royalty. I stand on a shrine all day while people stare up at me and admire me. I even have priests take care of me! They treat me so well and so carefully – almost like I'm made of porcelain!

The only thing is . . . well, it's actually quite boring. I can't talk to anyone, you see, because for some reason when I do, they immediately run screaming from the room! The other day I made the mistake of yawning and this poor woman actually fainted. FAINTED! Can you imagine?

I'm thinking of sneaking out into town tomorrow to get my hair done properly. I might even get some highlights. After all, a doll of my status deserves a little pampering session every now and then! The only problem is, I'm a doll. And dolls don't have jobs or money. I wonder if I can convince a priest to give me some . . .

Wish me luck!

Okiku, the Haunted and Fabulous Doll

RASPUTIN'S MYSTICAL POWERS

Chief Detectives, our next mystery to solve is all about the spooky figure of Rasputin, also known as the mad monk. Together we're going to find out whether or not he had mystical healing powers!

Rasputin's story takes place in Russia, a very large country that stretches from Eastern Europe to Asia. Russia is famous for many things, including really big, impressive books, ballet and being very snowy! At the height of his fame Rasputin lived in St Petersburg, which was then the Russian Empire's capital city. It was also home to the Romanovs, the Russian royal family.

→ TIMELINE →

1897 Rasputin is said to gain supernatural powers after a religious experience.

1905 Rasputin meets the Romanovs and soon becomes part of their inner circle.

1912 *Pious Reflections* is published, containing Rasputin's surprisingly accurate predictions of the future.

The Mysterious Monk

Rasputin was a religious man and mystical healer who became an important advisor to the last emperor of Russia, Tsar Nicholas II. He gained a very sinister reputation in his lifetime. This was mostly because of how close he became to the royal family, despite his humble background.

How did a man who was born to a very poor peasant family win such influence? Well, it was said that he gained supernatural powers after going on a religious journey to a monastery, and that he used those powers to heal. He soon became famous for it in fact. To this day he's still thought of as a monk, even though he was never actually part of the church!

Spooky Stories

There were many rumours and stories told about Rasputin. Some people even believed that he had a say in how the Russian Army fought in the First World War. But it's very hard to know what is true.

It was also said he had terrible manners and rarely washed, so he always smelled really bad – a mad monk with a bad funk!

So, Chief Detective, it's up to you to decide, did Rasputin have *supernatural* powers or was he just an ordinary man with a super-awful bath routine?

1912

Rasputin supposedly cures the tsar's son.

1914

The mad monk survives a near-fatal stab wound.

1917

Three months after Rasputin is finally killed in 1916, people claim to see him come back to life.

Turn the page to keep reading and find out about these events, and more!

THE EVIDENCE

Let's investigate! We're going to show you three pieces of evidence on Rasputin's mystical powers and then you can decide whether to Bust or Trust them.

FIRST PIECE OF EVIDENCE:

Alexei's 'miracle cure', 1912

Rasputin's miraculous 'cure' of the tsar's son, Alexei, is arguably what helped him become so powerful. Alexei suffered from haemophilia, a condition where the blood doesn't clot properly, so cuts or bruises take longer to stop bleeding. This means injuries can be very dangerous. Nowadays there are brilliant treatments for people with the condition, but at the beginning of the 20th century, haemophilia was still a mystery and no doctor had been able to treat the young Alexei.

When Rasputin came to see Alexei, he demanded all the doctors' medicines be thrown in the fire. After just one session, Alexei was much, much better – in fact, the tsarina believed her son was cured. Proof of Rasputin's special healing powers, surely!

Well, it's a great story but there is another possible explanation. Some historians have argued that doctors would have prescribed Alexei aspirin, a common medicine at the time.

But what doctors didn't know then was that aspirin makes it even harder for the blood to clot, so makes haemophilia much worse. By getting rid of all those bad medicines, Alexei's symptoms would instantly have got better.

SECOND PIECE OF EVIDENCE:

Pious Reflections, 1912

Our second piece of evidence is a little book Rasputin wrote called *Pious Reflections*. 'Pious' is a word that means 'religious' or 'spiritual'. This book was filled with predictions of the future and, amazingly, some of them DID come true!

Rasputin predicted the Russian Revolution of 1917 AND the death of the Russian royal family. In his book, he writes: 'Darkness will descend on Petersburg. When its name is changed [to Petrograd], then the Empire will end.' And five years later, that's exactly what happened! St Petersburg *did* become Petrograd when the Russian Revolution toppled the royal family.

HOWEVER, Rasputin's book also contained many predictions that *didn't* come true.

THIRD PIECE OF EVIDENCE:

Rasputin's death, 1916

The third piece of evidence is the fact that Rasputin could not be killed! Well, until he *was* killed. But it wasn't at all easy for the people who were trying to kill him!

In 1914, Rasputin was stabbed in the stomach by a peasant woman named Khioniya Guseva. He was so seriously wounded people believed he would die, yet somehow he survived.

Two years later, some Russian nobles decided Rasputin was too powerful and decided to get rid of him. They fed him poisoned cakes and wine, but nothing happened! So they ended up shooting him and throwing him into a freezing cold river in order to be sure that they'd finished him off. Talk about overkill!

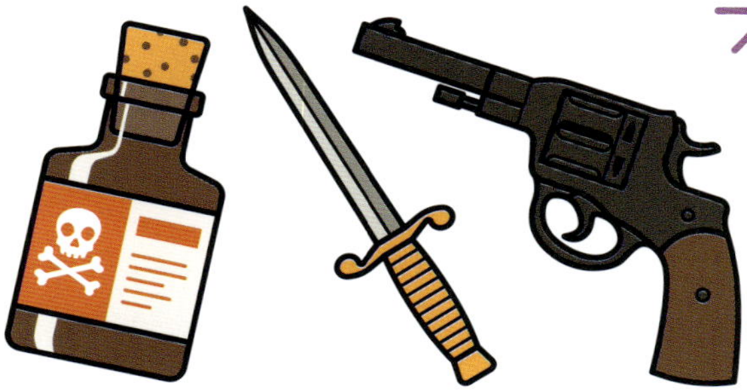

So, it seems Rasputin survived being stabbed and poisoned, and had to be shot *and* drowned before he finally died. Sounds pretty immortal, right? You know, apart from, er . . . the dying bit.

Okay, Chief Detective! Let's take a look at the evidence and BUST the whole idea that Rasputin had mystical powers.

THE MYTH BUSTER ARGUMENT

BUST ARGUMENT ONE:

Magic or medicine?

One of the biggest pieces of evidence for Rasputin's powers is how he supposedly healed Alexei using his mystical abilities. But as we've seen, it's possible that all he actually did was stop the doctors from making Alexei's condition worse. In fact, right up until he died, Alexei was *never* fully cured of his haemophilia.

In another famous story, Alexei was seriously hurt during a carriage ride. He seemed so close to death that his mother sent Rasputin a telegram asking him to pray for her son. Rasputin replied, 'Do not grieve, the Little One will not die. Do not allow the doctors to bother him too much.' Alexei's bleeding stopped the following day and the tsarina was even more convinced of Rasputin's healing powers.

But if you think about it, there's a very simple explanation for Alexei's recovery. By telling the tsarina to keep the doctors (and the aspirin) away, Rasputin gave Alexei's body time to heal on its own!

BUST ARGUMENT TWO:

Prophecy schmophecy

There's no doubt that Rasputin was spookily accurate with some of the predictions in his *Pious Reflections* book. However, he also predicted things that didn't happen, including that the First World War would be over quickly, which it wasn't, and that Alexei would take the throne.

One of his spookiest prophecies was when he predicted his own death at the hands of the tsar's relatives. However, he was a very disliked man and had a lot of enemies, so it's not surprising he could make a good guess about who might try to kill him. None of that means he was some sort of mystic psychic.

And Rasputin himself didn't actually call any of his writings 'predictions', more just theories of what might happen.

BUST ARGUMENT THREE:

Supernatural or super spooky?

Let's be honest, a lot of the details of Rasputin's assassination attempts are a bit sketchy. By all accounts the stabbing did happen, and it's amazing that in that day and age he managed to survive it. However, when it comes to the poisoning and drowning, the doctor who checked Rasputin's body said there was no poison in his system and no water in his lungs, meaning he didn't drown! It was the three gunshots that got him.

Also remember, all the stories about how hard it was to kill Rasputin came from the people who did the deed. It was in their interests to make him sound all supernatural and scary to make their crime look less bad.

THE MYTH TRUSTER ARGUMENT

Okay, okay. Buster makes some great points, but don't reach a decision just yet! Let's take a look at the Trust side of things.

TRUST ARGUMENT ONE:

Hypnotic healing

It's true that a lot of people now think Rasputin healed Alexei by stopping him from taking medicine that was making him sicker, but some historians think there could be another explanation. Historian Marc Ferro, for instance, believed that Rasputin was able to slow down or stop Alexei's bleeding by using hypnosis. This would make sense, as Orthodox priests in Russia were known to use hypnosis, and there's a good chance that Rasputin became familiar with the technique through them.

While there is modern scientific evidence to show that hypnosis can actually help haemophilia under certain circumstances, it still isn't fully understood. Seems pretty mystical to me!

TRUST ARGUMENT TWO:

Terrifying truths

Many of Rasputin's predictions were eerily true. One of his most accurate prophecies was about the fall of the royal family itself:

'Whenever, I embrace the Tsar and the Tsarina, the girls, and the Tsesarevich, I shudder with horror, as if I embrace the dead. And then I pray for these people. I pray for the Imperial Family, because the shadow of a long Eclipse falls on them.'

Haunting! And ultimately, he was right. The tsar and his family tragically lost their lives during the Russian Revolution. Rasputin also predicted both climate change AND cloning! Well, sort of. He predicted that human science would get so advanced that we would be able to start making animals. And this prediction kind of came true when Dolly the Sheep was successfully cloned in 1996. Either he was supernatural or super-smart!

TRUST ARGUMENT THREE:

Talk about overkill!

Not only was Rasputin very hard to kill, but even after his death there were still stories being whispered about him. Take this odd tale. In March 1917, three months after his death, Rasputin's body was placed onto a pile of logs and set alight to cremate him. A number of villagers came out to watch and almost every one of them swears they saw Rasputin's body rise up in the fire. Ooooh! Spooky!

Science *does* explain how a dead body can sometimes move when it's heated up, BUT isn't it also possible (and much cooler) to believe that the mad monk came back from the dead?

So now we're handing it over to you, Chief Detective. What do YOU think? Are you a 'NO WAY Rasputin had mystical powers' Myth Buster?

Or a 'Rasputin absolutely had mystical powers' Myth Truster?

WHAT DO YOU THINK?

Okay, Chief Detective, let's crack open this case and try to solve it with one of our detective skills. For this mystery, we're going to THINK IN GREY one more time.

CRACKING THE CASE

Let's start by reading the Detective Skill box on the right. Then, take a look at the scale below. On this scale, the black square is Bust and the white square is Trust, and the grey squares are somewhere in between.

BUST TRUST

Now, look at the statements below and see where you think each one comes in your scale. Do you 100% Bust it (black) or 100% Trust it (white), or is it more of a grey Bust or a grey Trust? Discuss your ideas with a friend or a grown-up.

DETECTIVE SKILL

Think in Grey

You may already be familiar with this Detective Skill from one of our previous cases, Bigfoot, but here's a reminder. Thinking in Grey is where instead of asking ourselves 'Do I believe this, YES or NO?', we ask ourselves '*How confident* am I that this is true?'

✦ **Rasputin cured the tsar's son** ✦

✦ **Rasputin was harder to kill than an ordinary person** ✦

✦ **Rasputin predicted the future** ✦

✦ **Rasputin's body came back to life on the fire** ✦

Finally ask yourself, in the case of Rasputin's mystical powers, are you **BUST** or **TRUST**?

RASPUTIN'S DIARY, 1 July 1914

Dear Diary,

First things first, it has come to my attention that some people are calling me smelly. Which is ridiculous as I wash my underwear at least once every six months! This morning the tsarina snuck me a whole plate of delicious sugary cakes for breakfast. I told her it wasn't very holy-man-like, but that didn't stop me from gobbling it all up! I only wish I could have had it with some wine though . . .

Later, the tsar came to me with a big frown on his face. Apparently, there's a massive war about to start. Yawn. Grown-up problems are so dull! But the tsar looked so worried that I ended up patting him on the head and comforting him with one of my famous prophecies. Ahem!

'Three hungry snakes will crawl along the roads of Europe, leaving behind ash and smoke . . .'

It didn't seem to brighten his mood though. Oh well!

You know . . . I'm beginning to think that maybe being a holy man isn't all prayers and potions. Maybe it's also about wearing smelly underwear, eating delicious cakes and telling creepy prophecies.

This palace life is way more difficult than people think!

THE LOCH NESS MONSTER

Our next case is a very famous one indeed: the Loch Ness Monster of Scotland, or Nessie as she is affectionately known. Most Nessie spotters say this legendary creature looks a bit like a snake or a long-necked dinosaur swimming through the water.

Rumours of a monster living in Loch Ness have floated around for centuries. There have been so many sightings over the years that Nessie has become a bit of an international legend, and people from all over the world visit Scotland just to catch a glimpse of her. In fact, according to the Loch Ness Centre, there have been 1,153 reported sightings of the lake-dwelling beauty. That's a lot of eyewitnesses!

TIMELINE

An Irish monk writes about a river monster.

6th century

A local newspaper reports the first modern-day sighting of Nessie.

1933

The first photograph of Nessie causes a stir.

1934

The What

The fascination we have with Nessie today really began in 1933 with an article in a Scottish newspaper called *The Inverness Courier*. In it, a local couple, Mr and Mrs Mackay, claimed to have seen something strange in Loch Ness. They said there was a large beast in the loch and described it as a 'whale-like fish'. People have been searching for Old Nessie ever since!

The Where

Scotland is one of the four countries that make up the United Kingdom, along with England, Wales and Northern Ireland. Scotland is famous for many things, including bagpipes, tartan kilts and haggis – a meal made from meat and herbs boiled in a sheep's stomach. But it's also known for having a lot of lakes, or lochs as they are known in Scottish Gaelic. There are thought to be over 30,000 of them, and some are enormous!

Loch Ness, where Nessie supposedly lives, is the biggest of all. It's roughly 36 kilometres long and contains over 7,000 million cubic metres of water, which is more water than all the lakes of England and Wales put together! It's also very deep, up to 230 metres in places. That's about the same as 2,000 soda cans stacked on top of each other. So, PLENTY of space to hide a swimming dinosaur!

Now it's up to you, Chief Detective, to join the search and see what you can find . . .

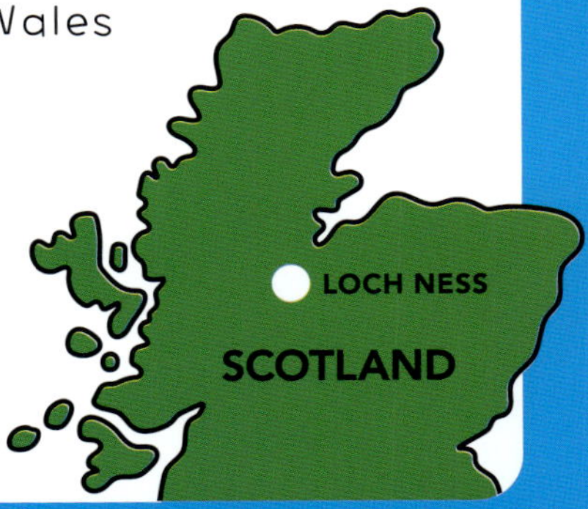

A holiday-maker snaps the most recent photos of Nessie.

2018

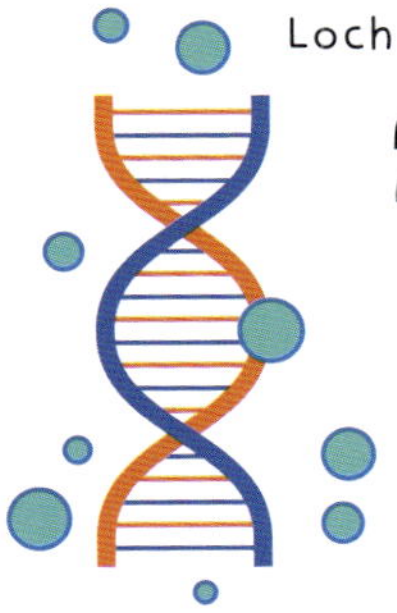

Researchers study DNA found in the Loch Ness water.

2019

Volunteers take part in the biggest ever Nessie hunt!

2023

Turn the page to keep reading and find out about these events, and more!

THE EVIDENCE

Okay, Chief Detective, time to take a *loch* at some splashing good evidence! Let's find out whether Nessie is a monster or a myth!

FIRST PIECE OF EVIDENCE:

Nessie photographs (1934–2018)

There have been LOTS of photos taken over the years of the Loch Ness Monster. And while many have been proven to be fake, there are many that still remain unexplained.

Arguably the most famous photo was taken in 1934 by Robert Kenneth Wilson, a London surgeon. It shows a long neck rising out of the water which looks a lot like a Brachiosaurus (a long-necked dinosaur). For 60 years the 'surgeon's photograph' (as it came to be known) was viewed by some as proof of Nessie's existence.

But in 1993, the photograph was studied for a TV documentary and it was discovered that the object in the image was actually quite small, under a metre long. As a result, the most famous photo of Nessie is now considered by most people to be a hoax.

The most recent photos of Nessie were taken in 2018 by a woman named Chie Kelly, who was on holiday with her family. Her photos are far clearer than the 'surgeon's photograph' and show something dark and snake-like in the water.

SECOND PIECE OF EVIDENCE:

DNA samples, 2019

In 2019, researchers in New Zealand looked at DNA taken from the Loch Ness water to see what lived there. (DNA is like a special code that's inside every living thing and can tell us a lot about different animals, people and plants.)

They said there was definitely no evidence of a prehistoric creature, but there was a LOT of eel DNA. Many scientists now believe that giant eels account for many, if not most, of the Nessie sightings. Some have pooh-poohed this *hypothesis* though, because eels roll from side to side like snakes – and that's just not how Nessie moves!

A *hypothesis* is an assumption or idea that must be tested to see if it is true.

THIRD PIECE OF EVIDENCE:

Unidentified noises, Nessie Hunt, 2023

In 2023, the biggest ever Nessie hunt took place in Scotland, organized by the Loch Ness Centre and a team called Loch Ness Exploration. Over 200 volunteers signed up to take part in recording and reporting any sightings that took place at Loch Ness over two days, and over 300 people watched a live stream of the event.

One boat of volunteers used underwater listening devices and picked up four unidentified 'gloop' sounds. However, they . . . er . . . forgot to turn their recording equipment on, so the sounds can't be studied! Elsewhere, cameras picked up a giant shadow moving just under the surface.

THE MYTH BUSTER ARGUMENT

So, Chief Detective, it's time to look over the evidence and decide what to believe. Are you a Nessie Myth Buster like me?

BUST ARGUMENT ONE:

Snappy snapshots

A lot of the supposed evidence for Nessie is based around the famous 'surgeon's photograph' of 1934 – but most people believe this photo to be a hoax. And since then, many other photos of Nessie have also been proven to be fake.

Here's an example. In 2011, a Loch Ness cruise boat operator called George Edwards took a photo that showed a blurry humped shape stranded in the middle of the loch. He even claimed that he sent the photo to the US to be analysed! Naturally, it got Nessie fans very excited. But later Edwards admitted that his photo was a fake. The hump was in fact a fibreglass model that had been created for a National Geographic documentary about the mythical beast.

All of this begs the question, if Nessie really exists, why have so many people gone to such lengths to make fake photos to trick us?

BUST ARGUMENT TWO:

Big Nessie besties

Chief Detective, you might remember the mysterious case of Bigfoot and the Bigfoot bias! Well, there might be something similar going on here with Nessie's besties.

It's worth noting that a LOT of Nessie sightings have been made by people who already believe the Loch Ness Monster exists. And so, their bias means they are more likely to find or see something. For example, the volunteers from the Nessie hunt in 2023 wanted to find something. And so they did!

BUST ARGUMENT THREE:

Loch at the science!

Over the years, there have been hundreds of different reported sightings of Nessie. Yet, the descriptions of the so-called monster aren't always similar! Some people describe a large snake, others a whale, a dinosaur, a lizard, or even a seal. Which just goes to show, the human imagination is a weird and wonderful thing!

The most popular image of Nessie is that of a prehistoric dinosaur. YET, when the waters of Loch Ness were tested, there was no evidence of dinosaur DNA in the water. What's more, Loch Ness has existed for only 10,000 years, but dinosaurs died out 65 million years ago. So a prehistoric dinosaur could never have lived in the lake.

So, if people aren't seeing Nessie, what are they seeing? There are plenty of other animals that Nessie could be, from eels to seals. When zoologist Jeremy Wade investigated the creature in 2013 for a TV series called *River Monsters*, he concluded that Nessie could actually be a Greenland shark. These sharks can reach up to 6 metres in length and live in the North Atlantic Ocean around Canada, Greenland, Iceland, Norway and POSSIBLY Scotland!

THE MYTH TRUSTER ARGUMENT

Okay, Chief Detective! It's true that Buster has made some excellent points. But let me present a few reasons why you should TRUST in Nessie . . .

TRUST ARGUMENT ONE:

Loch at it this way

Yes, there have been many photos of Nessie that have been proved false, but that doesn't mean that they *all* are. There are many that could still be real.

As well as Chie Kelly's photos, there is also a famous picture taken in 1955 by a holiday-maker named Peter MacNab. The photo shows what looks like a long snake, or at least something with a long neck, swimming beside the ruins of Urquhart Castle. One British national newspaper, *The Guardian*, has called the image 'one of the few to have withstood scientific examination'. And while the photo is old, black-and-white and a bit grainy, scientists haven't been able to prove that it wasn't Nessie.

And if you're not convinced by photos, how about actual film footage? In 2021, a drone being flown over the loch captured a long, thin form just beneath the water's surface. The mysterious shape only made a brief appearance, but maybe it was Nessie, caught on film!

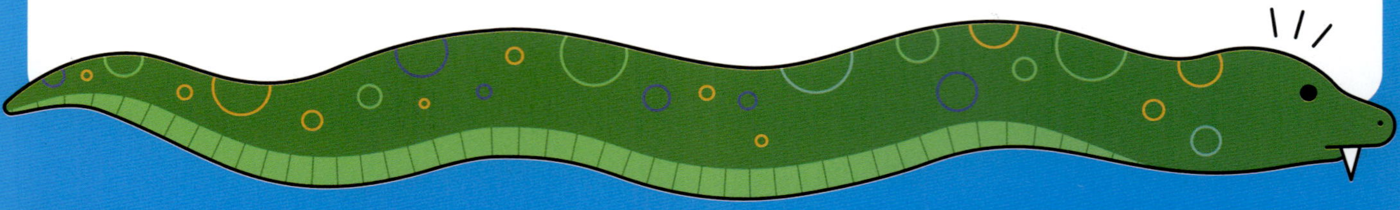

TRUST ARGUMENT TWO:

Old, old Nessie

The legend of Nessie only really became popular after the Mackays' sighting in 1933, but there have been several other accounts of a beast in Loch Ness, dating back 1,500 years!

The earliest report of a water monster shows up in an ancient text from the 6th century written by Saint Columba, an Irish monk. In it, he describes hearing a monster while staying near the mouth of the River Ness. After kindly sending one of his companions to check out the river, he saw the monster with his own eyes and promptly banished it.

Surely it's a bit too much of a coincidence for the same type of creature to have been seen in the same place over the course of centuries?

TRUST ARGUMENT THREE:

Hide-and-water-seek!

Exploring underwater is no easy task. As already explained, Loch Ness is HUGE – it holds enough water to fill more than two and a half million Olympic-sized swimming pools! Plus, the soil that washes into the lake from nearby hills makes the water really dark and murky. With all that water to hide in, is it really surprising that Nessie has been able to stay out of sight for so long?

Okay, Chief Detective, now it's time to BUST this case wide open. Do you think Nessie is a myth, like me?

Or are you a Myth Truster, like me? Because monsters can get camera-shy!

Come on Nessie, if you're there, take some selfies and help us out!

WHAT DO YOU THINK?

Okay, Chief Detective! You've seen all the evidence, so let's use a detective skill you've already explored to decide whether to Bust or Trust Loch Ness Nessie. It's time to EVALUATE TESTIMONY again!

CRACKING THE CASE

For each of the witnesses below, ask yourself whether you think they're telling the truth, lying or making a mistake.

✦ 6th century: Saint Columba (written account) ✦

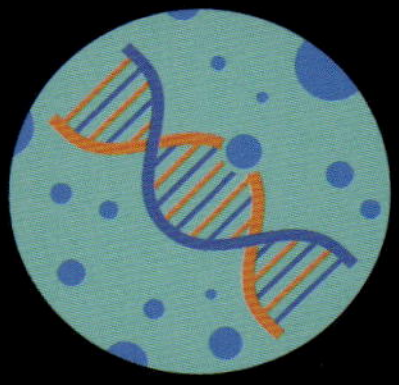

✦ 2019: New Zealand scientists (DNA analysis of water samples) ✦

✦ 2023: Volunteers on the Nessie hunt (strange sounds) ✦

You could think about some of these questions: Might the witness be biased? Did they have anything to gain from spotting Nessie? Is the witness an expert? Don't be afraid to get others involved in the discussion!

Once you have weighed up the witnesses and decided which ones you believe, ask yourself, in the case of the Loch Ness Monster, are you **BUST** or **TRUST**?

DETECTIVE SKILL

Evaluate Testimony

Most of the time we think people are either telling the truth or lying, right? But there is actually a third option! Suppose that you're sure that you saw your friend at the park, so you confidently tell someone else that they were there. However, you later discover your friend was actually away on holiday. This means that you weren't telling the truth, but you weren't lying either. So, when we're trying to figure out if someone is telling the truth we need to consider three possibilities: they're telling the truth, they're lying, or they're honestly mistaken.

BUST! TRUST

It’s just another day at Loch Ness for Greenland sharks Ethel and Geraldine . . .

So Geraldine, what's the first rule of Really Wild Swimming Club?
We don't forget our towels.
Very good. And the second?
Don't talk about Really Wild Swimming Club or everyone will take all the good spots.
Correct! Now, have you practised?
Yes, I think I'm ready! So, we start with a back tuck somersault, then we scull for 5 seconds, do a side fishtail, turn . . .
Then I lift you up out of the water for the classic Nessie photo shot and . . .
Huge underwater monster blob shape! Hahahaha!

Look, it's Nessie!

Later that day . . .

Wow! I can't believe we did it! I want to go to the championships. Let's go, please Ethel.
Lake Erie here we come! My Aunt Bessie swam there, you know?

TRUST ! BUST

PLACES

THE LOST CITY OF ATLANTIS

Our next Bust or Trust case will really WET your appetite as we're taking a deep dive into the legendary story of the Lost City of Atlantis, an ancient kingdom that reportedly sank beneath the waves more than 10,000 years ago.

The name 'Atlantis' is Greek. Translated, it literally means 'Atlas's island'. Nowadays, an atlas is a book of maps and charts – which is funny considering Atlantis isn't on any maps and has never been found!

Atlantis was first mentioned around 360 BCE by a Greek philosopher named Plato. Plato was born almost two and a half thousand years ago. That's a really, really long time! Philosophers are people who spend a lot of time thinking about the world and asking questions about life. There were a few world-famous philosophers in Ancient Greece and Plato was one of them.

TIMELINE

According to Plato, the ancient kingdom of Atlantis sinks beneath the waves.

Around 9600 BCE

The Minoan civilization is wiped out by a volcanic eruption.

Around 1150 BCE

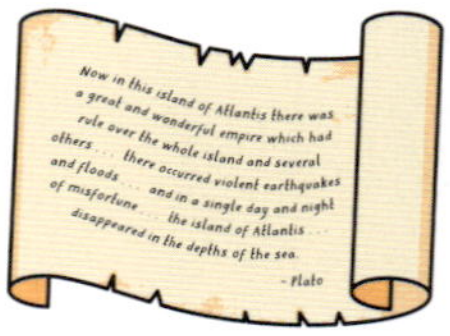

Plato writes about Atlantis.

360 BCE

The Myth

Plato described Atlantis in such incredible detail that people have been talking about it ever since! According to Plato, Atlantis was a powerful civilization on an island in the Atlantic Ocean. The people were wise and noble, and the island was rich, full of beautiful fruits and metals. But when Atlantis became greedy for more power, the gods sent earthquakes and floods to punish it, and eventually the island sank beneath the sea.

The Modern-day Legend

Atlantis has inspired countless books, stories, poems, games and movies over the years – and some pretty wild theories! Some people think that it might have been swallowed up by the Bermuda Triangle, a strange area of the Atlantic Ocean where boats and planes are said to completely disappear . . . Another theory is that Atlantis drifted south and became the icy continent of Antarctica!

Explorers have been trying to locate the lost kingdom for hundreds of years, BUT did it even exist in the first place? Chief Detective, it's up to you to decide: was Atlantis a real-life place or just a soggy myth?

The strange Antikythera mechanism is discovered in a shipwreck off the coast of a Greek island.

1901

A TV documentary claims to have found evidence of Atlantis.

2017

Satellite images capture what look like the remains of a temple – right where Atlantis was believed to be.

2018

Turn the page to keep reading and find out about these events, and more!

THE EVIDENCE

Okay, Chief Detective, we're going to present you with three pieces of evidence. Then it's up to you to decide if Atlantis really existed or if it is just a watery tale. Let's Bust or Trust!

FIRST PIECE OF EVIDENCE:

The works of Plato, 360 BCE

As we mentioned, the first person to write about Atlantis was Plato, who described it in two separate works named *Timaeus* and *Critias*. His descriptions were incredibly detailed and sounded very real.

BUT he was writing about an island that supposedly disappeared almost 8,000 years before he was born! So, how could he possibly know about it? Perhaps it was just a story? But if so, Plato never says that he made it up.

> Now in this island of Atlantis there was a great and wonderful empire which had rule over the whole island and several others . . . there occurred violent earthquakes and floods . . . and in a single day and night of misfortune . . . the island of Atlantis . . . disappeared in the depths of the sea.
>
> – Plato

SECOND PIECE OF EVIDENCE:

Anchors found during *Atlantis Rising* documentary, 2017

The second piece of evidence is pretty cool because it's a *physical* piece of evidence – you can actually see it and touch it! But ONLY if you're able to get a boat to the Strait of Gibraltar (that's in the Atlantic Ocean near Spain and Morocco) and dive deep, deep down under the sea.

In 2017, two famous movie directors, James Cameron and Simcha Jacobovici, decided they would try and find Atlantis as part of a documentary film called *Atlantis Rising*. The team studied Plato's writings and calculated that Atlantis must lie off the Strait of Gibraltar. So they organized a dive to try and find evidence of the lost kingdom.

AND THEY FOUND SOME! Six ancient anchors to be precise. Simcha Jacobovici reckoned they could be 4,000 years old.

However, Atlantis is supposedly 10,000 years old, not 4,000. Of course, Plato might have just got his dates mixed up.

THIRD PIECE OF EVIDENCE:

Satellite images, 2018

In 2018, a company called Merlin Burrows decided to use satellite images to see if they could uncover Atlantis. Their search led them to the Doñana National Park in Spain, an area of wetland north of the Strait of Gibraltar, which is . . . really close to where the *Atlantis Rising* team found the anchors! Coincidence? Maybe not!

The satellite images showed large circles that could have been the bases of huge towers, as well as the ruins of what may have been a temple. There were also signs that the area might once have been hit by a tsunami, which ties in with the story of Atlantis sinking beneath the waves.

Merlin Burrows say they took samples from the ruins, which showed that they were human-made and between 10,000 and 12,000 years old – exactly the right age for Atlantis! BUT they didn't explain what they used to study the samples, which means no one else could check their claims.

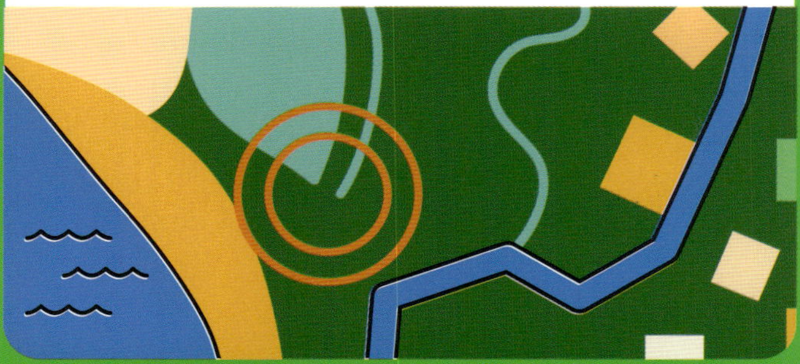

THE MYTH BUSTER ARGUMENT

Okay, Chief Detective, let's take another look at the evidence and see if Atlantis really existed. Let's Bust this Greek bubble!

BUST ARGUMENT ONE:

Where in the world?

Plato's description of Atlantis is very detailed, but some of those details seem VERY fantastical! For example, he describes Atlantis as being larger than Libya (part of North Africa) and Asia put together, which implies it was pretty big! So for it to have vanished completely is a bit unlikely.

In fact, most historians and scientists believe that Plato's account of the lost kingdom of Atlantis was entirely fictional. They think that the Greek philosopher invented Atlantis to be a cautionary tale of the gods punishing human greed. Plato was famous for using *allegories*, which are stories that are used to teach a certain lesson.

And this makes sense, because outside of Plato's tale, no other written records of Atlantis exist. There are lots of other texts from Ancient Greece, yet Atlantis isn't mentioned once. Talk about fishy!

BUST ARGUMENT TWO:

Atlantis by any other name . . .

Here's another theory for you, Busters. What if Atlantis never existed and was just a story inspired by the real-life destruction of another island?

The Minoans were an ancient people who lived in Crete (a Greek island) from around 5,000 years ago. Their civilization had many advanced skills, including art, sailing, writing, and building great cities filled with beautiful palaces. Much like Atlantis!

Then, about 3,600 years ago, disaster struck. A volcano on another Greek island, Santorini, erupted, causing a huge earthquake, large dust clouds and tsunamis. Over the years, several more earthquakes and eruptions followed, and the great Minoan civilization was eventually wiped out. Maybe its destruction inspired Plato's story?

BUST ARGUMENT THREE:

Murky waters

The fact is, for all the little things that have been discovered under the sea, no great sunken civilization has ever been found.

Cameron and Jacobovici might have found some very old anchors, but they didn't find any other evidence. And even if you believe Merlin Burrows' claim that ruins in Doñana National Park were built by humans 10,000 years ago, it doesn't mean the site is definitely Atlantis. Several civilizations have been lost to natural disasters or, er, angry gods over the years. Just like the Minoans!

THE MYTH TRUSTER ARGUMENT

Buster makes some great points, but there's still time for Truster to turn the tide and persuade you to believe that Atlantis was real!

TRUST ARGUMENT ONE:

Greek-ish geography

Yes, it's true that it's a bit strange for an entire island to go missing, especially if it was as big as Plato described. That being said, Plato wouldn't have known the *real* size of Asia and Libya.

When Plato was writing, the Ancient Greeks had not explored much of the world and only knew about the lands closest to them. Greek maps, like the one shown here, were made based on the words of a Greek man called Herodotus, who described the world in around 450 BCE. So, when Plato said Atlantis was the size of Asia and Libya, he actually meant it was the size of an area of land much smaller than Europe. This might explain why Atlantis has never been found. It was still a big island – just nowhere near as big as Plato thought!

TRUST ARGUMENT TWO:

Anchors away

Remember the anchors that were discovered in the Atlantic Ocean? Let's not forget just how close they were found to where Plato claimed Atlantis to be – just off the Strait of Gibraltar, on a site where there is now no land at all, but where an island port could have existed a long, long time ago.

It's true that there were no other signs that a kingdom had once been there. BUT arguably a kingdom is exactly what was found the following year in Doñana National Park, which is only around 350 kilometres away from the dive site. Think about it, TWO pieces of Atlantis evidence found very close to each other in the exact location described by Plato! Surely that's not a coincidence?

TRUST ARGUMENT THREE:

Advanced attitudes!

Finally, we have some extra evidence for you to consider. Plato described the Atlanteans as having advanced technologies for their time, right?

Step forward the Antikythera mechanism. This odd, metal device was found on a very old shipwreck off the Greek island of Antikythera. It's thought to be a sort of ancient computer that is over 2,000 years old. Apparently it was designed to calculate the positions of the stars, planets, Sun and Moon. But what is so interesting is that it was very smart for the time – no one else was making anything else like this. Perhaps the people who made it were using skills that were passed down from an advanced society . . . like Atlantis?

So now we're handing it over to you, Chief Detective! Do these theories about the Lost Kingdom of Atlantis hold water?

Or do they just give you a sinking feeling? Are you an Atlantis Myth Buster?

Or an Atlantis Myth Truster?

WHAT DO YOU THINK?

Right, Chief Detective, now you've heard all the evidence, let's put a detective skill to the test. For this mystery, we're going to WEIGH THE EVIDENCE once again!

CRACKING THE CASE

Okay Detective, first read the Detective Skill box on the right, then grab a pencil and some paper and carefully look through all the evidence and make two columns. In one column, write down all the evidence we have that Atlantis really existed. And in the other, write down all the evidence that it did not exist.

Is there more evidence for or against? Or is it about even?

Now, use a scale from 1–10 to grade each piece of evidence for its quality, where 1 means 'This isn't very likely at all' and 10 means 'I believe in this so much!' Count up the points from each column. Which one has more points?

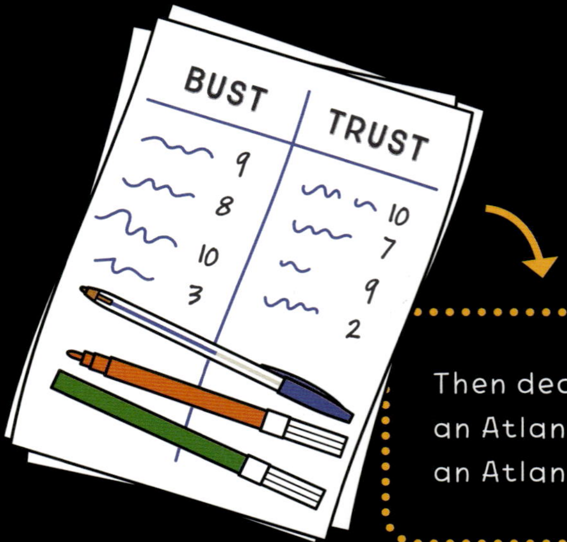

Then decide, are you an Atlantis **BUSTER** or an Atlantis **TRUSTER**?

DETECTIVE SKILL

Weigh the Evidence

Remember, there are two things to look at when weighing evidence:

1. **Quantity of Evidence:** This is how much evidence we have.

2. **Quality of Evidence:** This is how reliable or trustworthy the evidence is.

Both the quantity and quality of evidence help us figure out whether or not we should believe in something. However, it's worth saying that if the evidence is of a very poor quality, then it might be that no amount of it can ever be enough!

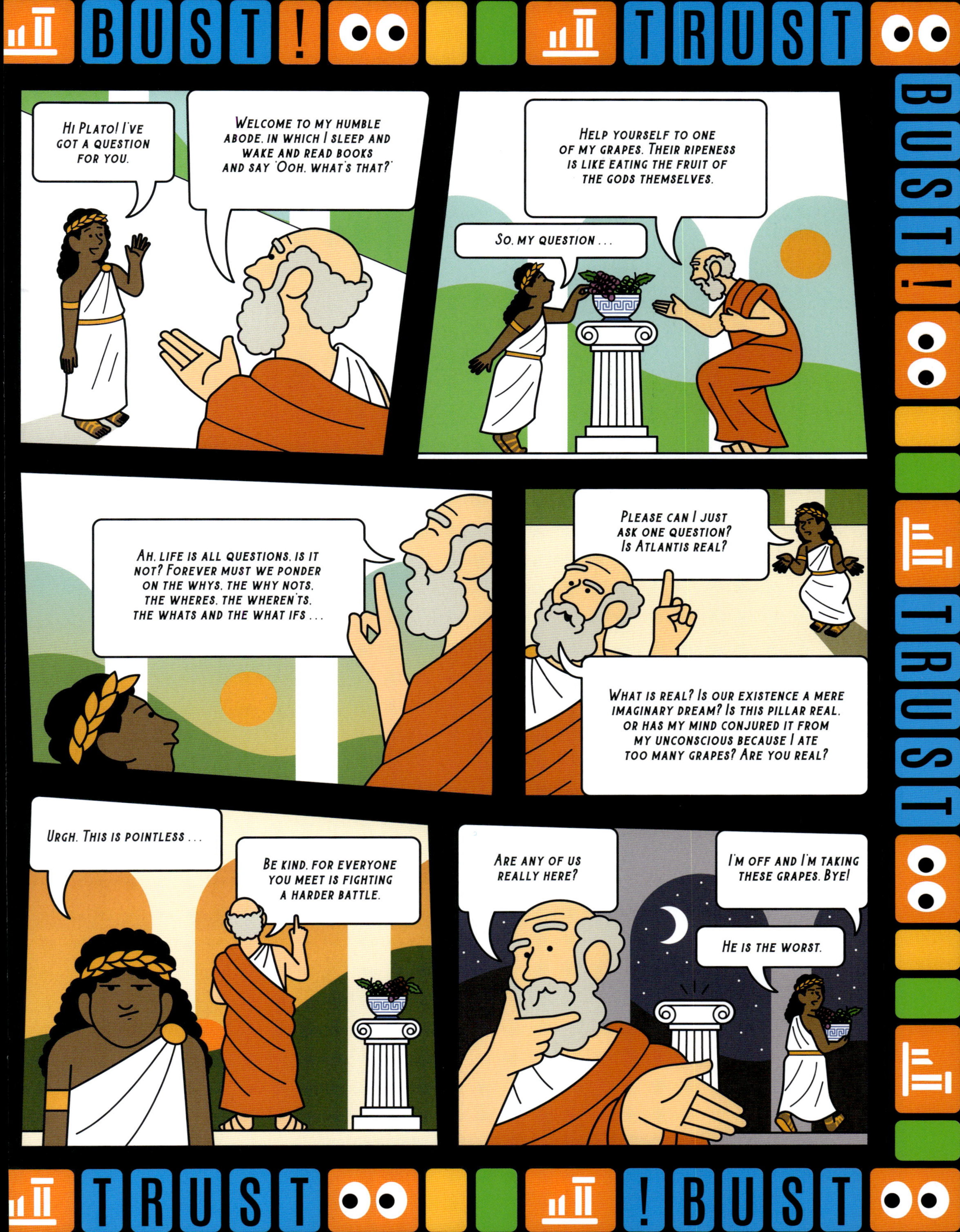
HI PLATO! I'VE GOT A QUESTION FOR YOU.
WELCOME TO MY HUMBLE ABODE, IN WHICH I SLEEP AND WAKE AND READ BOOKS AND SAY 'OOH, WHAT'S THAT?'
HELP YOURSELF TO ONE OF MY GRAPES. THEIR RIPENESS IS LIKE EATING THE FRUIT OF THE GODS THEMSELVES.
SO, MY QUESTION . . .
AH, LIFE IS ALL QUESTIONS, IS IT NOT? FOREVER MUST WE PONDER ON THE WHYS, THE WHY NOTS, THE WHERES, THE WHEREN'TS, THE WHATS AND THE WHAT IFS . . .
PLEASE CAN I JUST ASK ONE QUESTION? IS ATLANTIS REAL?
WHAT IS REAL? IS OUR EXISTENCE A MERE IMAGINARY DREAM? IS THIS PILLAR REAL, OR HAS MY MIND CONJURED IT FROM MY UNCONSCIOUS BECAUSE I ATE TOO MANY GRAPES? ARE YOU REAL?
URGH. THIS IS POINTLESS . . .
BE KIND, FOR EVERYONE YOU MEET IS FIGHTING A HARDER BATTLE.
ARE ANY OF US REALLY HERE?
I'M OFF AND I'M TAKING THESE GRAPES. BYE!
HE IS THE WORST.

THE CRYSTAL SKULLS

The next case is the head-scratching – or rather *skull*-scratching – Mystery of the Crystal Skulls. Some have claimed these spooky artefacts were made by the Ancient Maya and have special powers!

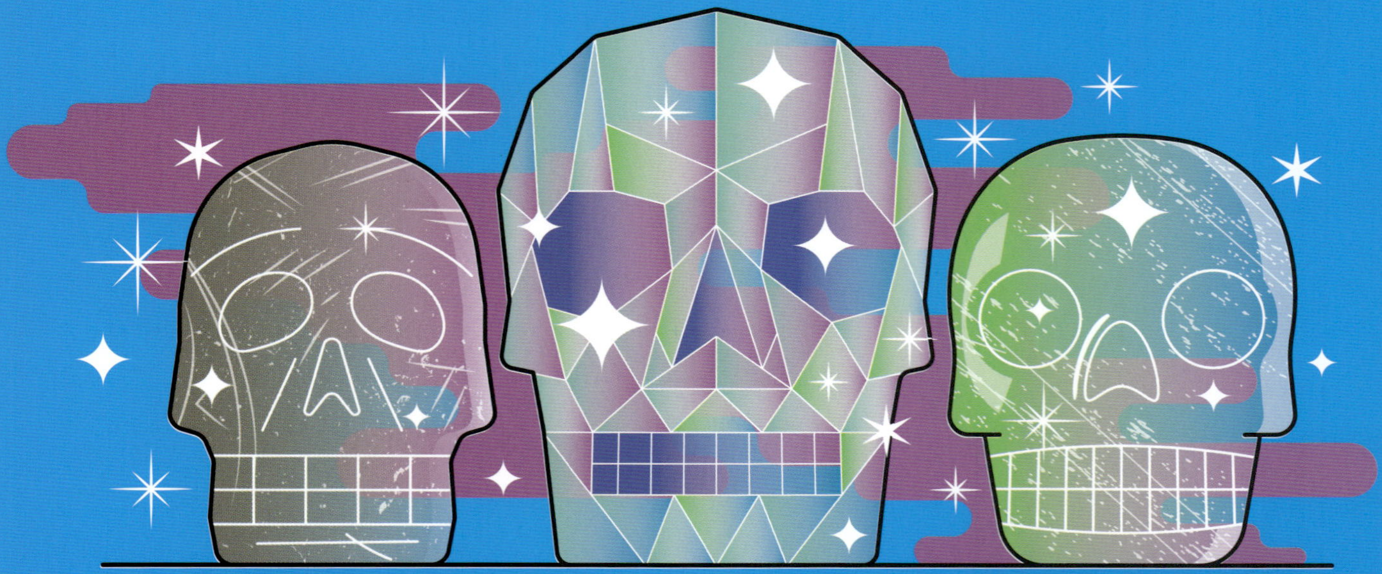

The crystal skulls are 13 carvings of human skulls, made from a clear or milky type of crystal called quartz. The skulls have found their way into museums across the world, and inspired many books and films, including *Indiana Jones and the Kingdom of the Crystal Skull*. But there's a big mystery behind them: no one knows for sure where they came from!

TIMELINE

1800s

Eugène Boban sells several crystal skulls to collectors.

1924

A father and daughter claim to have found the Skull of Doom in a temple in Central America.

1970s

Art expert Frank Dorland examines the Skull of Doom.

From Maya to Museums

The most famous crystal skull is known as the Skull of Doom. It was supposedly discovered in 1924 by a young woman and her father in the ruins of a Maya temple in Central America. The Maya were a civilization that existed for thousands of years. They are known for their sophisticated writing system and advanced understanding of the stars.

There are also 12 other crystal skulls. Some of these were sold to collectors in the late 1800s by Eugène Boban, who was an *antiquarian*, which is someone who studies or deals in old objects. He frequently travelled to Mexico to buy antiquities to sell in his shop in Paris. One of the skulls he sold even ended up at the British Museum in London.

Super Skulls

Not everyone believes the skulls were made by the Ancient Aztecs or Maya. Some people say they may have been left on Earth by aliens, or that they are ancient artefacts from the lost city of Atlantis. (Remember Atlantis?) It is also claimed that the skulls have special powers. Some people have even suggested that they are a form of computer and the history of the world is stored inside them!

There are also plenty of people who believe that the skulls aren't ancient at all, have no special powers and are just one big hoax.

Now, Chief Detective, it's up to you to decide for yourself whether to BUST or TRUST that the crystal skulls are powerful ancient objects with special powers.

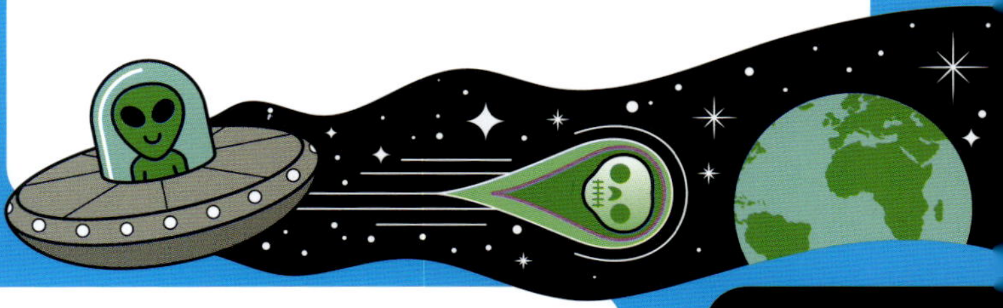

Anthropologist Jane MacLaren Walsh performs tests on the Skull of Doom.

2007

The British Museum and the American Museum of Natural History publish a study of the crystal skulls in their own collections.

2008

A facial reconstruction of the Skull of Doom is done for a documentary.

2011

Turn the page to keep reading and find out about these events, and more!

THE EVIDENCE

Okay, Chief Detective, we're going to show you the evidence and then you can decide whether you believe in the power of the crystal skulls, or whether you think it's all just skullduggery!

FIRST PIECE OF EVIDENCE:

F. A. Mitchell-Hedges's autobiography, 1954

Anna Mitchell-Hedges claimed to have found the Skull of Doom in 1924 in the ruins of a temple in Belize, a country in Central America. Her father, who was a well-known British adventurer called Frederick Albert Mitchell-Hedges, described the discovery in his 1954 autobiography. In the book, he claimed that the skull was at least 3,600 years old and was used by Maya priests when performing certain rituals mainly to do with, well, death. Hence its creepy name!

However, Frederick *also* wrote in a letter to a friend that he'd bought the skull at an auction in 1943. An auction is a place where people buy and sell things. And if that's true, it *wasn't* found in the ruins of a temple in Belize!

Of course, even if the skull *wasn't* found in a Maya ruin, that doesn't mean it's not ancient.

SECOND PIECE OF EVIDENCE:

Examinations of the Skull of Doom, 1970s onwards

Let's look at what experts have said about the Skull of Doom over the years.

In the 1970s, the skull was handed to art restorer Frank Dorland. His job was preserving and repairing old works of art. Frank thought the skull had been made without metal tools and had probably been carved using diamonds over a period of 150 to 300 years. He also estimated that it could be 12,000 years old.

Then, in 2007, the skull was investigated by Jane MacLaren Walsh, an anthropologist at the Smithsonian Museum in the USA. Anthropologists are people who study humans of the past and present. Jane's tests showed it had almost certainly been made with a high-powered metal tool, probably in the 1930s – a long time after the Maya were around!

Finally, in 2011, forensic artist Gloria Nusse used facial reconstruction for a documentary. That's when computers are used to show what the face of a skull's owner would have looked like when they were alive. It found that the skull was modelled on a European woman from the last 200 years, so it couldn't have been made by the Ancient Maya!

THIRD PIECE OF EVIDENCE:

Accounts of the skulls' powers

Now, on to the legendary powers of the crystal skulls! There are two skulls that are actively used to help people.

First, there is the skull known as Max, which was supposedly discovered in Guatemala. It is said to have healed a number of people who have touched it and meditated next to it. Then there is the skull Sha Na Ra, found in Mexico in 1995. Its owner charges a fee for sessions with it.

And let's not forget the Skull of Doom! Anna Mitchell-Hedges claimed her skull gave her visions of the future and also had the power to kill – scary! Scientists, though, say there is no evidence that any of the crystal skulls have any powers.

Okay, Chief Detective! Let's take a closer look at the evidence and see if I can convince you to Bust the myth, like me.

THE MYTH BUSTER ARGUMENT

BUST ARGUMENT ONE:

Maybe not Maya!

The biggest mystery of the crystal skulls is that no one knows exactly where they came from or who made them. But one thing we DO know is that they're not thousands of years old.

You've already heard how Jane MacLaren Walsh investigated the Skull of Doom and decided it had probably been made in the 1930s. Well, in 2008, the British Museum and the American Museum of Natural History published a study about the crystal skulls in their own collections. They used special microscopes to look closely at the skulls and found markings that proved they could only have been made with modern carving tools. Both museums guessed that the skulls dated back to sometime in the mid- to late 1800s.

Later, the British Museum said it believed that the skulls could be traced to a place in Germany famous for manufacturing small quartz and crystal designs in the late 1800s. So if the skulls were made in Germany, they can't be Maya!

BUST ARGUMENT TWO:

Bamboozling Boban

Let's talk about Eugène Boban – remember him? In the 19th century, he sold at least five different crystal skulls to collectors, all of which are now displayed in museums around the world.

But one thing you need to know about Eugène Boban is that he became quite famous for selling fake artefacts to museums! In fact, he was a very tricky man, who made many museums gain his trust by telling them that he was an expert in Mexican history and could help them to spot any fakes. But of course, what he actually did was sell them fake objects, while insisting they were the real deal.

So, it's very likely the crystal skulls he was selling were fakes too. Still, this doesn't explain where he got them from, and maybe no one will ever know for sure!

BUST ARGUMENT THREE:

Fake folklore

One of the most popular stories about the crystal skulls is the legend that if all 13 are brought together in one place, it will give the owner great power. This legend supposedly comes from Native American folklore.

It's a great story! But there's one problem: there's no evidence at all that there's even been a prophecy like that in Native American folklore. In fact, no one seems to have heard of this 'legend' at all until the 20th century. Don't forget, too, that scientists have said there's no evidence the crystal skulls have any special powers.

THE MYTH TRUSTER ARGUMENT

Okay, Chief Detective! Let's see whether I can persuade you to Trust, like me, that the crystal skulls are powerful ancient objects!

TRUST ARGUMENT ONE:

The original skull-finding father-daughter duo

Let's take another look at Frederick Mitchell-Hedges and his daughter, Anna. It's true that Frederick told a friend he bought the Skull of Doom at an auction. But maybe this was a lie. After Frederick Mitchell-Hedges passed away, his daughter Anna took the skull around the world. She continued to tell the original story of how she and her father found the skull underneath an altar in a ruined temple – and she never once changed her story for the rest of her life. So, maybe she was telling the truth?

TRUST ARGUMENT TWO:

Healers & believers

No matter where the skulls came from, there are plenty of people who believe in their powers.

You've already heard about the skulls called Max and Sha Na Ra, which are said to heal people. JoAnn Park, the person who looks after Max, says that the skull is 'here to help and guide each individual who's come into contact with him to find peace, harmony and forgiveness within one's self.' Plenty of people believe Max does just that.

And they're not the only ones who believe there's something strange about the skulls. Do you remember the art restorer Frank Dorland, who examined the Skull of Doom? Well, he claimed to have heard music and bells coming from it. Spooky! Maybe the crystal skulls really DO have powers?

TRUST ARGUMENT THREE:

Powers out of this world!

One crystal skull was found by a family in Guatemala in 1909, and in 1991 it somehow found its way to Joky van Dieten in the Netherlands. Joky is a 'spiritual adventurer' who says that the crystal skull cured her of a really horrible illness. She takes it all around the world to help cure people of problems.

Joky calls the skull 'ET' as it looks like the alien in the famous film from the 1980s. And get this, Joky doesn't just believe her skull *looks* like an extraterrestrial – she believes that it actually IS extraterrestrial! She thinks the skull arrived from some stars that are 444 light years away.

And who knows, perhaps she's right! Plenty of people believe in aliens, including clever space scientists. So maybe the real answer to the mystery of the crystal skulls lies out of this world . . .

So, Chief Detective, what do you think? Are you still a bit uncertain?
Or do you think the truth is CRYSTAL clear? (Get it? Ha ha!)

WHAT DO YOU THINK?

Alright, Chief Detective, let's put these crystals under the microscope and use some of our detective skills! For this mystery, let's do some more INDEPENDENT RESEARCH.

CRACKING THE CASE

Now it's time for you to do some research of your own! With a grown-up, see what OTHER evidence you can find about the crystal skulls. This might mean reading books or searching the internet for articles, videos or podcasts that support or challenge the myth.

Grab a pen and paper and record any new pieces of evidence you find. Can you figure out what kinds of evidence they are?

✦ Are there people who saw something happen? (Eyewitnesses) ✦

✦ Did a scientist or historian say something important? (Testimony) ✦

✦ Did you find any objects or photographs in your research? (Physical evidence) ✦

Finally, ask yourself if you **BUST** or **TRUST** this evidence? Does it change your mind about the mystery?

DETECTIVE SKILL

Do Independent Research

Here's a reminder about how to find reliable information online. Remember that this must always be done with a grown-up.

1. **Use Reliable Sources:** Trustworthy sources include news and school websites or books from school libraries.

2. **Cross-check Information:** Compare the information you find to other sources. If there are opposite views, investigate further to decide which is more reliable.

3. **Be Critical:** Question where information comes from. Ask questions such as: Who created this content? Is the evidence of good quality?

Diary of a Crystal Skull, Day 567

Dear Diary,

It is now day 567 of being kept in this glass box. Every day, people come and press their gawking faces against the window of my prison. They have such odd fur on top of their heads and such dull skulls – they don't shine at all!

Today, someone in a white lab coat dared to disturb my peace. The creature removed me from my glass prison and poked and prodded at me with strange tools. I really wanted to bat them away – but sadly I do not have arms, so it was rather impossible.

To spite them, I decided to shine extra bright. After all, it must be awful for them, not being able to glow the way I do. Perhaps they will envy my brilliance and set me free.

Until tomorrow,
Crystal Skull – Masterpiece of Nature

In 1992, the Smithsonian Museum received a mysterious crystal skull. Someone sent it without leaving a name. Today the Smithsonian Skull can be found on display at the National Museum of Natural History, Washington, D.C.

THE DEMON DANCING PLAGUE OF EUROPE

Our next case is all-singing and all-dancing! We're about to solve the mystery of the demonic dancing plague of central Europe. Let's boogie into the case and bust some myths while we bust some moves!

The dancing plague was a strange series of events that happened in Europe in the medieval period, a time also known as the 'Dark Ages'. It involved groups of people dancing uncontrollably without stopping for days on end!

Sounds like the ultimate party, right? Well, the dancing was a fair bit more dangerous than the name suggests. People would dance until they were unable to eat or sleep, and some even danced themselves to death!

→ TIMELINE →

A large group of children dance their way across Germany.

1237

People in Aachen (in modern-day Germany) start dancing as if possessed.

1374

The famous dancing plague begins in Strasbourg (in modern-day France).

1518

Dancing Mania

The dancing plague began in July 1518 in Strasbourg, Alsace (which is now in France). It was called a plague because it seemed to be contagious – which means that it seemed to spread from person to person. Well, they do say that rhythm can be infectious!

Around this time, huge groups of people were dancing in the streets all over central and western Europe. It's thought that somewhere between 50 and 400 people took to dancing for weeks. Yet just a few months after it started, the dancing plague stopped.

A Medieval Mystery

There were lots of theories at the time as to what caused this strange, groovy plague. In the medieval period, many people in Europe used religion and spiritual beliefs to explain things they didn't understand. So a lot of people believed that the dancers had been possessed by demons, or bad spirits, which were controlling them and making them dance.

Wait a second, freeze pose! Nowadays, we know a lot more about science, the human body and the way people think, and so there are other theories to explain the dancing plague. Ones that are far less . . . possess-y!

Now it's your job to decide, was the demon dancing plague, well, demonic? Or was it something less supernatural? Come on, Chief Detective, let's Bust or Trust!

Mass laughing is reported in Tanzania.

1962

Outbreaks of mass crying and shouting happen on and off across Nepal.

2016–2018

Groups of people start mass screaming in Malaysia.

2019

Turn the page to keep reading and find out about these events, and more!

THE EVIDENCE

Okay, Chief Detective, we're going to dance through the evidence with you and then you can decide whether the demon dancing plague was magic or mania!

FIRST PIECE OF EVIDENCE:

Eyewitness accounts, 1518

'[They] formed circles hand in hand, and appearing to have lost all control over their senses, continued dancing, regardless of the bystanders, for hours together, in wild delirium, until at length they fell to the ground in a state of exhaustion.'

– *The Black Death and The Dancing Mania*
Justus Friedrich Karl Hecker

'Both men and women were abused by the devil to such a degree that they danced in their homes, in the churches and in the streets, holding each other's hands and leaping in the air . . .'

– Peter of Herental (a monk)

The first pieces of evidence are the witness statements that described what happened to the people who caught the plague. These eyewitness accounts certainly make it sound like the dancers were possessed, don't they?! It doesn't make any sense to dance so much that you hurt yourself.

However, at that time it was pretty common to believe in demons and possessions. People often blamed things they didn't understand on evil spirits. So it's not surprising that many witnesses believed they were seeing a demonic dance.

SECOND PIECE OF EVIDENCE:

Exorcism ceremonies, 1518

The next piece of evidence is how the dancing plague ended. Back in 1518, the main cure for something as strange as this was a special ceremony called an 'exorcism'. This was carried out by people of the church to remove bad spirits, and it seemed to work! According to Peter the monk, the dancers 'were freed of their demons by means of exorcisms'.

Why would a ceremony to remove demons work, if the dancing plague wasn't caused by demons? Well, Peter's account might be biased – he was a monk and so would be very likely to believe in exorcisms, considering that he was part of the church.

THIRD PIECE OF EVIDENCE:

More dancing outbreaks, 1237 & 1374

The final piece of evidence is the fact that dancing outbreaks have happened on multiple occasions in several different countries over many years.

In 1374, almost 150 years before the dancing plague in Strasbourg, people on the streets of Aachen (in what is now Germany) began dancing uncontrollably. Within weeks, the dancing fever had spread to the Netherlands and France.

And if we go back even earlier in time, there was another strange outbreak of dancing mania in 1237, where a large group of children travelled almost 20 kilometres across Germany, jumping and dancing the entire way. This story became so well-known that it's thought to have been the inspiration behind the popular tale of the Pied Piper!

What could have caused all these weird episodes of dancing mania? Maybe something supernatural was at play.

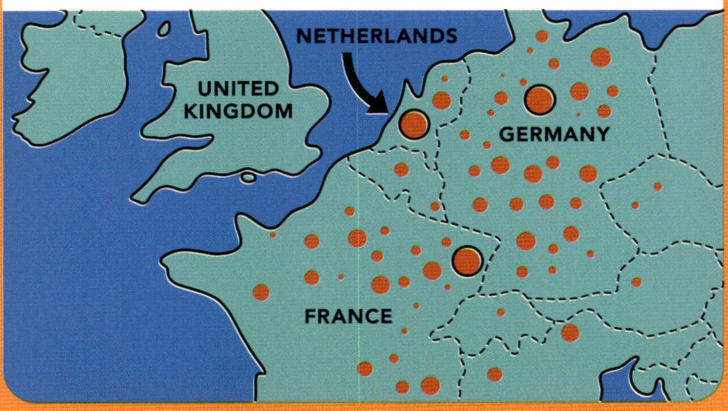

THE MYTH BUSTER ARGUMENT

Okay Detective, let's have a look at the evidence, and see whether you're a demonic plague buster, like me!

BUST ARGUMENT ONE:

The Devil's bread

One of the strangest theories about the dancing plague is that it was caused by ergot poisoning. Ergot is a type of fungus that most commonly attacks the rye plant, which we use to make bread. Symptoms of ergot poisoning include confusion, strange visions, spasms and convulsions, which is when the body moves all by itself.

Ergot poisoning is now thought to be behind a lot of the old tales of witchcraft, and modern scientists and historians think it could explain the demon dancing plagues as well. Can you imagine? Bread that makes you dance! Luckily, ergot poisoning is really rare today because we carefully test all our food.

BUST ARGUMENT TWO:

Mass madness & dancing feet

John Waller, an American medical historian, believes that the dancing plague was a form of mass psychogenic disorder. This term is the name for physical illnesses that are caused by extreme emotional or mental stress.

Most of the outbreaks of dance fever took place during the medieval period, a time when life was very hard – it wasn't called the Dark Ages for nothing! It is very possible that the uncontrollable dancing was brought on by the pressures of living in such an unstable and difficult time, when awful things such as famines and terrible diseases were happening all around. Perhaps all the stress got too much for some people and dancing was their way of expressing it?

BUST ARGUMENT THREE:

From belief to BUSTING moves

Another theory, also put forward by John Waller, is that the dancing plagues only happened in places where people *already believed* in dancing curses. Studies have shown that people are more likely to experience 'possessions' or trances if they already believe in the possibility of spirit possession.

The dancers in 1518 definitely lived in a time where divine curses and possessions seemed like real and true threats. The people of Strasbourg believed in Saint Vitus, who was the patron saint of epileptics and dancers. To them, it would have seemed perfectly believable that Saint Vitus had given them a dancing curse!

The dancing plagues happened mostly during the medieval period and continued right up until the beginning of the time known as the 'Enlightenment'. During the Enlightenment, people in Europe started to question the cause of bad things that happened to them, and instead of blaming evil spirits, they began to think about other explanations, like science. Think about it: isn't it suspicious that when people stopped *believing* in demonic dancing, the dancing outbreaks stopped?

THE MYTH TRUSTER ARGUMENT

Wow, there are some really funky facts there! But let's have a look at some more TRUST-worthy arguments.

TRUST ARGUMENT ONE:

Spirit eviction

The council of Strasbourg tried lots of different ways of curing the dancing plague, from setting up big halls with musicians so that the dancers had somewhere safe to dance, to banning public dancing and music entirely. However, these efforts didn't actually cure that many people.

But the cure that *did* seem to work was sending the dancers to the shrine of Saint Vitus to be exorcised. There, the dancers were made to wear red shoes, which were sprinkled with holy water and painted with crosses. Apparently this ritual led Saint Vitus to 'forgive' the dancers, and the dancing plague soon ended.

Of course, some might say this was a matter of belief – the people *believed* that the church had cured them, and so they stopped dancing. BUT, it could also be true that Saint Vitus really did forgive the dancers and the church had come up with an effective cure!

TRUST ARGUMENT TWO:

Modern-day manias

It's true that there haven't been any more cases of mass dancing since the medieval period. BUT there have been similarly strange cases in more recent times, including – get this – an event of mass laughing in Tanzania in 1962, mass screaming in Malaysia in 2019, and mass crying and shouting in Nepal between 2016 and 2018! All of these cases struck schools first, before spreading further out into the community. Spooky, huh?

There were stressful things going on in each place when the outbreaks took place, so that has been the explanation given for most of them. But you can't deny it all sounds rather supernatural, doesn't it?

TRUST ARGUMENT THREE:

Demons & doubt

The fact is, the real cause for the dancing demon plague is still unknown. Yes, there are lots of theories, from bread poisoning to mass hysteria, but no one can say with 100 per cent confidence that it *wasn't* caused by demons.

Just think about it: people danced for several days, with bruised and bloodied feet. Some of them kept on dancing until they dropped down dead! That can't have all been from eating some dodgy bread, can it? Something more supernatural must be at play!

So now we're handing it over to you, Chief Detective.

What do YOU think? Are you a demon dancing plague Myth Buster?

Or a demon dancing plague Myth Truster?

WHAT DO YOU THINK?

Right, Chief Detective! We're going to waltz our way through this case, using one of our handy Chief Detective skills: CHECK FOR PERSONAL BIAS.

CRACKING THE CASE

First read the Detective Skill box on the right, then ask yourself the following questions:

✦ **What do you *want* to believe about the demon dancers? Would you rather they were possessed or not?** ✦

✦ **Now think carefully, do you think this influences what you believe?** ✦

Give yourself some time to consider this. Sometimes it's difficult to see our own biases! Now put yourself in the demon dancers' shoes, and ask yourself:

✦ **What do you think the dancers believed in 1518? Did they believe in curses?** ✦

✦ **Do you think that their beliefs influenced how they behaved?** ✦

Now decide, are you **BUSTING** or **TRUSTING** the supernatural demon dancers?

DETECTIVE SKILL

Check for Personal Bias

Do you remember how we talked about 'bias' or 'motivated reasoning' in the Okiku the Haunted Doll mystery? Bias is when what we *want* to believe influences what we *do* believe. Feelings can often become facts in our heads! So it's important to try and look at things from as many different points of view as possible.

BUST! TRUST
Whoa, I'm so tired. My legs are so achy. This is awful.
Hey! You ok?
No! I've got the dancing plague. I've been dancing for seven hours now and I just can't stop.
Ah, hang on a second . . .
Oh wow, I've stopped dancing! What happened?
I just gave you the pass-the-parcel plague.
I can't help myself, I have to unwrap it really quickly! Yippee, I got a sweet!
Now quick, pass it on!
WOW, this is fun!
Yeah, it's fun for a while, but I've been unable to stop myself unwrapping parcels for four days now. In a minute I'm heading over there.
What's going on over there?
They have the birthday-cake-eating plague. For the first few slices it's great, but then it gets a bit much – there's a lot of icing!
BUST! TRUST
TRUST !BUST

DETECTIVE DICTIONARY

ALLEGEDLY – this word means that something hasn't been proven.

BIAS – bias is when what we *want* to believe has an influence on what we *do* believe.

COINCIDENCE – where similar or related events happen at the same time by chance and without any planning.

CRITICAL THINKING – the act of questioning our own opinions and using reason to solve problems.

EVIDENCE – information that gives you a reason to believe something is true.

EYEWITNESS – a person who has seen something happen and can tell others about it.

FRAUD – tricking someone, usually to make money.

HEARSAY – information that you have heard but do not know to be true.

HOAX – when someone is tricked into believing something to be true.

HYPOTHESIS – an assumption or idea that must be tested to see if it might be true.

SUPERNATURAL – something magical that can't be explained by science.

SUSPECT – to suspect something is to have an idea about something or to believe something could be true.

TESTIMONY – a formal statement from someone about what they know or what they have seen or heard.

THEORY – an idea or set of ideas that is intended to explain facts or events.